For Bad Bear,
with every good wish
for you to have a
happy Father's Day!
My best,
Sharon Brikman Fiske

Praise for *The Birkman Method*

"It's critical to know the things that make a person tick. Once you understand the individuals you work with each day, you can give greater opportunity to your employees and create a more powerful team. *The Birkman Method* is an easy read that provides thought-provoking insights and understanding."

—**Steve Lufburrow,** CEO,
Goodwill Industries of Houston

"The Birkman Method is a tool that provides awareness, understanding, and wisdom for anyone on a learning journey. The power of the Birkman is its ability to make sense of the stories we tell of our interactions with others, which forms the basis of who we are and how we act. This wonderful book shares these stories so that all can relate."

—**Kelly D. Bean,** assistant dean, UCLA
Anderson Executive Education

"Beliefs and perceptions are such dangerous things—they can cost you so much. The Birkman Method helps me recognize them in myself and in others, but more important, it provides a framework for talking about them in an open, nonconfrontational way. I simply don't know what I would do without the Birkman."

—**Justin Parer,** managing director,
Pi Strategic Management

"The Birkman Method's unique approach sets it apart from any other psychometric assessment tool. Eleven years and 4,500 completed assessments later, we continue to rely on it to add value to our company's individual development and team-building efforts on an ongoing basis."

—**Margie Poole,** senior organizational development consultant,
CenterPoint Energy

"Building strong leaders and exceptional teams are table stakes for competing successfully in our industry. The Birkman Method has been an invaluable tool for us in supporting this mission for an extended period of time."

—**John Farrell,** senior director of organizational development,
Marathon Oil Company

The Birkman Method

YOUR PERSONALITY AT WORK

Sharon Birkman Fink
Stephanie Capparell

JB JOSSEY-BASS™
A Wiley Brand

Library of Congress Cataloging-in-Publication Data

Birkman Fink, Sharon, 1950–

The Birkman method : your personality at work / Sharon Birkman Fink, Stephanie Capparell—First edition.

pages cm

Includes bibliographical references and index.

ISBN 978-1-118-20701-7 (cloth); ISBN 978-1-118-41937-3 (ebk);

ISBN 978-1-118-42111-6 (ebk); ISBN 978-1-118-63759-3 (ebk)

1. Birkman Method of Personality Testing. 2. Personality. 3. Psychology, Industrial. I. Capparell, Stephanie. II. Title.

BF698.8.B47F56 2013

155.2'83—dc23

2012049928

Printed in the United States of America

FIRST EDITION

HB Printing 10 9 8 7 6 5 4 3 2 1

To Roger W. Birkman,
a man of vision whose genuine love for people
inspired him to spend a lifetime
perfecting a way for each of us
to see our full potential
and work together in harmony

Contents

Preface

Understanding and retaining people is most often cited as the number one challenge in business, and the top question leaders ask is: How do we hire, manage, and retain our people? While running a business may be hard, it turns out that managing people is even harder.

This is the reason people turn to the Birkman personality assessment: to improve their lives and their working relationships with those closest to them. For more than six decades, millions of individuals have used our positive-psychology tool in over fifty countries, and our client list has grown to include Fortune 500 companies, nonprofit groups, educational and faith-based organizations, mom-and-pop shops, couples, and families. As CEO of Birkman International, I receive e-mails daily from consultants around the world and across the United States.

The story of the Birkman Method begins with the story of my father, Roger Birkman. Growing up as the shy and thoughtful son of a Lutheran pastor, he was fascinated by people and a keen observer of them. As a B-17 bomber pilot during World War II, he saw the power of wide-ranging personal perceptions and the impact of different styles on people and their behaviors.

Returning from the war, he was swept into the booming field of social psychology. Alongside such figures as Benjamin Fruchter, Warren Bennis, and Abraham Maslow, my father was a pioneer in taking psychology to the workplace, a radical new concept at the time. He developed the Birkman Method by asking a variety of workers questions about themselves and how they did their jobs. These interviews of people in the workplace, from salesmen and truck drivers to janitors and top executives, formed the basis of his positive-psychology questionnaire, first called "A Test of Social Comprehension."

By the 1960s, my father, who always loved technology, put the research data from his test takers' responses on an IBM mainframe computer. These data enabled him to expand into the global workplace, tracking generational changes as well as shifting trends. Most important, the information shows how all individual employees shape corporate cultures and fit into a grander scheme.

But my father didn't do it alone. Soon after returning from the war in 1944, he was fortunate to meet a young woman in the Women's Army Corps at a Veterans Administration picnic. Margaret Sue Leath shared his passion for understanding people and believed in his mission from the beginning. They married a year later, and she worked alongside him until her death in 2007.

My early childhood memories include night after night of sitting at the dinner table listening to my parents talk about their work. Perfecting the Birkman assessment was their dream and a passion that consumed them. Every night my father pored over stacks of index cards filled with numbers and phrases, looking for patterns of behavior in the day's test takers. He often discussed his ideas and the results with my mother. I don't remember them talking about much else. At a time when few moms worked outside the home, my mother began to assist my father full time on Birkman research, and I started day care at age two. Since my preschool principal was a musical theater performer who loved music, she took me to audition (successfully!) for the role of the child in *Madame Butterfly* at Houston Grand Opera. From this experience at age five, I developed a lifelong love of music, just like my violin-playing mother did, that led to my first career: singing and working in opera and musical theater. From this point, much of my life focused on music and raising my three children.

Because my parents lived and breathed their Birkman work, my sister and I stayed closely involved in the family business. My dual careers in music and the Birkman Method were intertwined from the start, and I loved them both. In fact, stage directing and teaching voice gave me a chance to practice the team-building and coaching skills that the Birkman assessment encourages. Just as one off-key voice can ruin a scene, one out-of-sync attitude can derail a team or sabotage a whole production.

By 2001, I was ready to pick up my parents' torch and we began a planned leadership transition. I became CEO in 2002, and in the decade since, we've added 60 percent, or nearly 1 million people, to our database; boosted our overall revenues by almost 40 percent; and more than doubled the number of countries with Birkman consultants. We've trained hundreds of certified consultants, both corporate clients and independent practitioners, and expanded our research department to include psychometricians who have enabled us to update our career reports and develop a comprehensive new cognitive assessment, the Birkman Abilities Inventory. We were awarded the Texas Family Business Award in 2010 from Baylor University's School of Business and have continued to grow at a healthy rate each year.

What I understand today is the enduring value of what my parents started more than sixty years ago. Although it has taken a lifetime of effort and investment to perfect, my parents believed from the start that they had an excellent tool to measure social expectations, self-perception, interests, and stress behavior in a way useful to individuals and organizations. My goal is to continue their legacy and, more than anything else, to witness the wonders that happen when people replace defensiveness with appreciation, and confusion with understanding.

My great-great-grandfather arrived in Texas from Germany in the 1850s with our family name, Birkmann, which translates to "birch-man." Birches thrive only if they grow in relationship to at least one other birch tree or in a group of birches. The birch tree cannot thrive in isolation and will not flourish if it stands alone, and neither can any of us. The Birkman Method works because it looks at the potential of each individual *in relationship* to others, both as person-to-person and as person-to-team, to help us to identify the powerful, underlying needs and the strengths that shape our performance and contentment at work.

March 2013   Sharon Birkman Fink
Houston, Texas

The Birkman Method

Introduction

All of us have strengths, all of us have passions, and all of us have something that motivates us to succeed. And all of us have a particular work style that lays a path to that success. Because of that, all of us have value—something to contribute to our workplace, family, and community.

This understanding is at the core of the Birkman Method, a workplace assessment designed to identify and optimize your individual potential by teaching a healthy self-awareness and a greater understanding of how you might fit into the bigger picture of society. Once you achieve this insight, you are better able to identify your own strengths and get others to respect your needs, as well as help you to acknowledge the strengths of your colleagues and close associates.

The success of every workplace depends on the people in it and their relationships with others. Business happens through healthy connections with colleagues, bosses, direct reports, and the public—and with a certain level of comfort with the physical and emotional environment of the workplace. In the quest to find the key to such productive relationships, a mythology has been built around the workplace: the notion that certain personalities fit best in certain industries, that each profession requires a narrow set of skills, and that there are ideal qualities for leadership roles.

The Birkman, as we refer to it, disproves those misconceptions person by person. Instead, it offers a no-nonsense way to deal objectively with all types of personalities in all aspects of a job. It can give you concrete tips for every aspect of your life at work, from its special segment on how to talk about yourself in a job interview to suggestions for your boss on how to coach you based on your profile results. The assessment doesn't measure skill levels, character, or experience, but it reveals what can foster and make best use of all those attributes. After all, you don't have to be a great artist to appreciate great art. A fine-arts business needs an accountant, an engineering firm needs to sell its products, an oil conglomerate needs a human resource expert, and every business employs strategists and designers in some capacity. But these diverse needs aren't always apparent to everyone in those businesses.

The Birkman is the only assessment tool that reaches beyond mere self-described behavior to reveal the underlying motivations that drive and inspire you. The evaluation begins with a multiple-choice assessment that gives a richly layered profile of your interests and needs. It highlights vital aspects of your personality such as your relationship with authority, your response to incentives, and your ability to deal with change. Just as important, it flags triggers for stress that can derail your best efforts. Ultimately it fits all of these pieces into a clear context of how you see the world.

Roger W. Birkman, designer of the Birkman tool and a pioneer in the field of workplace psychology, said, "The reality of life is that your perceptions—right or wrong—influence everything else you do. When you get a proper perspective of your perceptions, you may be surprised how many other things fall into place."[1]

Purchasers of this book have access to a free Birkman assessment at http:www.birkman.com/book to take and submit electronically to Birkman International of Houston, Texas. There is more information on this in chapter 1. Once your results are processed, you will receive a brief personal profile by e-mail. You don't have to take the assessment first to glean the valuable leadership, workplace, and lifestyle lessons presented in this book. But reading the book with your own information in hand will lead to a fuller understanding.

There are no wrong answers to the Birkman assessment and no profile trait or work preference deemed unfit or in conflict with a productive setting. Instead, your resulting assessment profile will give you valuable insights into your workplace and interpersonal relationships.

The Birkman will help you reveal some basic truths about yourself—for example:

- How well do you accept direction and authority?
- How good are you at relating to individuals or groups?
- What are your most basic needs for motivation and reward?

Then it drills down deeper:

- Do you like to be spoken to in the same manner in which you speak to others, or is your public style very different from your personal needs?
- How do you really relate to individuals? You think you're fair, but are you in fact impatient with others' needs?

- You might have little artistic talent, but do you have a strong enough attraction to the arts that not indulging in them makes you feel out of sorts?
- How well do you take criticism?
- How critical are you of yourself?

It then aims to define your most productive work environment:

- Is your best work done during brief periods of intense focus or when you can take the time to think things through?
- How much variety do you need in your workweek?
- Do you need strong leadership, or are you a self-starter?
- You know you like the outdoors, but how does that affect your demeanor in the office?

The answers may not be what you expect. You may find, for example, that you appreciate a strong authority figure although you think of yourself as a self-starter, or that despite being very sociable, you need considerable time alone to recharge. The understanding begins when these questions are asked in an objective, unemotional way. It is expanded when others in your circle participate in the assessment. Its value can be enhanced by counseling by certified consultants should you decide to explore broader uses of the Birkman after you finish reading this book.

The Birkman profile is so sharply focused that those who have repeated the test decades apart typically get nearly identical results. You'll wonder how your responses to the Birkman led to such accurate and comprehensive conclusions.

Dr. Birkman began to craft his assessment tool in the 1950s. In the decades since, it has grown to become one of the most sophisticated measures of individuals' motivational needs and core interests. If similar approaches offer snapshots of employee types, the Birkman analysis unravels the DNA of workplace relationships, job satisfaction, and accomplishment. And like DNA profiles, its strength is in its huge database that allows comparative analysis with other testers, situations, and problems. By 2013, Birkman International had amassed the results of surveys taken by some 3 million people worldwide. No other similar evaluation maintains similar research data.

The Birkman translates well—literally—around the world. The assessment is offered in twenty-two languages under the guidance of some three thousand consultants worldwide. In settings representing all of those languages, the Birkman has been used to bridge cultural gaps for multinational companies and organizations. Clients say that it is practical, easy to understand, and insightful and that it has had a positive impact on their professional and personal lives.

People tend to be good at what they love and love what they are good at doing. The best careers therefore are built on passionate interests. But do you have a clear idea of what those are for you? You know what holds your interest, but have you figured out what you need to keep that interest over a long career or what simple steps you can take to change your workplace from frustrating to fulfilling?

For Birkman consultant Todd A. Uterstaedt, based in Cincinnati, the Birkman Method is a coaching tool with an important wider mission. "I love to show people they are so much more than the sum of their limitations and the box they are put in," he says. "The Birkman helps them reveal that in a kind and nonjudgmental way."

The Birkman approach focuses on individuals and can help you navigate the full spectrum of a rich career, beginning with pointing to possible work paths. Once you are on the job, it can show you how to reduce conflict and improve job relationships while fulfilling your personal needs. If you are a rank-and-file employee, it can show you how to avoid workplace minefields and grab success. It can answer why one staffer is clashing with another. (Often differences in work styles are misinterpreted as deliberate disruptions.) It also can point to why an employee with a solid history of achievement suddenly seems to be floundering. (Perhaps it's a change of environment that would be insignificant for one person but untenable for another.) Or why such a well-crafted team of talented people can't seem to get along. (Often motivational needs of an individual in a group are in conflict with the wishes of the whole.)

For C-suite executives, the assessment aids leadership development by pointing to strengths and exposing behavior that is unproductive. It can help bosses see the disparate needs of their many reports. It has been used to plot strategy for the most challenging negotiations. Results also have helped pull together teams by mapping out a group's diverse needs. Perhaps most important, it promotes diversity in the broadest sense of the word by identifying the valuable contributions of everyone who works together. By the end of the process, a company will have achieved productive harmony on the job, fueled by more inspiring leadership, and higher individual achievement.

In this book, we share stories of trainers and clients, protecting the privacy of certain individuals where appropriate. Readers will recognize themselves, and their colleagues and bosses, in dozens of examples of problem solving that range from helping some of the biggest corporations smooth dysfunctional relationships to showing small business entrepreneurs how to avoid money-wasting mistakes in hiring. It also presents case studies and anecdotes tied to particular workplace issues at the end of each chapter in "The Birkman at Work" sections.

You will meet an executive who snagged a record-breaking government contract after she used the Birkman to create a project team to lead a bidding competition with world-class rivals. At another multinational, a Birkman consultant helped one veteran executive realize that the leadership style that helped him achieve his considerable success suddenly wasn't working, as well at a time when he had to be more forward thinking. Another consultant had such rapid and dramatic success helping an airline union negotiate a labor contract that the union let management borrow him for strategic planning.

The Birkman has even been used at the end of a career to help design a retirement lifestyle. It has been adopted by life coaches, couples counselors, religious groups, family counselors, and civic organizations, including a prisoner release program. In recent years, the Birkman has been used by students in high school, college, graduate, executive MBA, and open enrollment programs, as well as in professional programs at a number of institutions, including Harvard Business School.

It is no wonder, then, that business clients also have asked that the Birkman be brought into their homes. One executive said that after receiving his Birkman feedback, he took his report home, handed it to his wife, and told her, "Here is my owner's manual."

BIRKMAN BEGINNINGS

Why have personality surveys like the Birkman become so ingrained in corporate culture? And why do so many corporate leaders remain passionate about the importance of this and other training tools? General Electric, for example, spends $1 billion annually worldwide on training and education programs for its employees. Its website states, "The results can be measured in the increasing leadership capabilities of our own people and ultimately in the value and opportunity generated for our customers and their communities."

These assessments were born in the post–World War II American idealism that government, academia, and corporate America were going to work together to rebuild the country to make it a better and more inclusive place. Thousands of U.S. veterans were reentering society and going to school on the GI Bill. Companies that were suddenly expanding and modernizing were in critical need of talent.

The task that social scientists faced after the war was as exciting as it was daunting. They aimed to reshuffle the whole of the American workforce and to do it in a way that would advance society and commerce. "The early 1950s would soon be stereotyped as an age of zombies in gray flannel suits, but it was actually a period of enormous social change and optimism, especially for the emerging middle-class," wrote Warren Bennis, professor of business administration at the University of Southern California. "For those as fortunate as I was, it was a downright giddy time. As social scientists, or would-be social scientists, we believed we had the tools to uncover the secrets of human behavior."[2] Dr. Birkman was one of those enthusiastic pioneers in industrial-organizational psychology. After the war, where he had flown as a B-17 fighter pilot, Dr. Birkman worked with the Veterans Administration giving aptitude tests to veterans using the GI Bill to help them discover what might be their best choice as a college major. "They wanted to know where to begin their destiny," he said. At the same time, American corporations were faced with the prospect of hiring a massive body of workers more diverse, more empowered, and more worldly than the country had ever seen before.

In Houston, Dr. Birkman processed sky-high stacks of veterans' files. He told veterans to work with their hands, or major in something to do with numbers, and other simple directives depending on how they answered some questions. "It was a beginning, but it was a huge beginning," he says. "They were behind the eight ball because the government was spending a lot of money sending veterans to college, and what were they going to get out of it?"

These veterans sitting in front of him with their remarkable life experiences had tales of leadership, valor, challenge, pain, and survival. Their potential was huge, important, and worthwhile. Veterans like Dr. Birkman, who had experienced war firsthand, saw again and again examples of how the person you least expected rose spectacularly under fire and how some of the most average inductees after training became superior leaders. He was determined to do better by them with a test and follow-up that would be broader, more meaningful, and more systematic, and from that point on he had a clear vision of his own future career. "I was thinking, there sure is a need in this area," he remembers. "People don't get into good positions haphazardly."

Dr. Birkman began to create an assessment tool, and by the time he received his doctorate from the University of Texas in

1961, he had nearly forty clients from his work on his dissertation, "Development of a Personality Test Using Social and Self-Perception Inventories." The government and corporate leaders embraced the efforts of academics such as Dr. Birkman. It was, after all, an era when science was king. Dr. Birkman and this group of men—and an unusual number of women for the day—held onto their idealism. As their numbers grew and diversified, they became instrumental in the following decades in the integration of African Americans and then women into the workforce at the professional level.

In 1967, Dr. Birkman put an end to the laborious colored-pencil hand-scoring of his tests and purchased an IBM mainframe—the 1401 IBM—to store the data. It proved to be a brilliant move: no rival personality assessment company has amassed such a big and historic data bank to this date.

Because of this massive database, Birkman consultants are often ahead of the curve in spotting business trends or interpreting changes in various fields. As the changing workforce has become more diverse in every way, these consultants have found little difference in responses related to gender, age, ethnicity, or other such markers. Birkman also has charted a smaller-than-expected difference in overall test scores among nationalities worldwide. While certain unique behaviors and customs are taught in different cultures, the more important underlying motivation and needs that drive people are shared around the globe. In other words, we humans are more alike than we realize, more similar than we are different. There is consistently more diversity within any one group than there is among groups.

There will always be something stronger that informs behavior at the foundation of any person, Dr. Birkman says.

"They give it different names, and you can combine the items and spin it a bit, but human nature is human nature and what runs through all of that is that once we learn something about the United States in depth, we've learned a lot about India and China in depth. It all goes back to the heart. And once you get that into the conversation, there is universal understanding."

The complexity of that human heart is fascinating and challenging. Around the world, the workplace—its physical location and its space on the Internet—is replacing the community as the gathering place for people and the place in which they seek fulfillment. Its allure is its vibrancy and its diversity, which has been the focus of the Birkman and its multicolored paradigm for personalities.

Yet the age-old questions remain: What makes a good employee? What makes a good boss? How can we work together to achieve common goals? Today in a workplace that has been radically transformed and expanded, the answers are becoming ever more complex—and more surprising too.

"So, does anyone else feel that their needs aren't being met?"

1

You Are Here!

Taking the Birkman

When we come to know and accept ourselves, we become free to accept others and appreciate how they complement us. At the heart of the Birkman Method is the philosophy that you have to treat people the way they want to be treated in order to help them become comfortable, confident, and able to function at their best.

This may sound logical, but it goes against our own instincts, which tell us that the conclusions we came to from our own vast experiences are what are normal and right, that what we need is what everyone else needs, that what led us to success will surely lead others there, and that the way we want to be treated is the way everyone else wants to be treated. It's the Golden Rule, after all. But people are complicated. Not only do they behave in ways that are contrary to our preferred actions, but they also act in ways that contradict even their own apparent styles. This is because our outward behavior doesn't always reflect what we need inside from others. Often our behavior was made to conform long ago to a standard demanded by our work or other social pressures.

The Birkman is a guide to how to get others to help us meet our true needs in exchange for our doing the same for them. If we can accomplish this, we can become our best selves, do our best work, and help others do the same. When the Birkman is introduced to members of a group that interact with each other in the workplace or any other setting, it opens a new dialogue that is more nurturing for each individual's interpersonal needs.

A common Birkman anecdote about the need for improved understanding and communication is hearing a client say, "I thought the person I worked with was trying to get under my skin to get ahead of me, but after I saw that person's Birkman, I understood it was just another perspective. It had nothing to do with me."

TAKE MY GOOD SIDE

You might ask about the Birkman questionnaire, "What are you going to assess: me at work, me at home, or me with friends? If it's work, will it show how I act in front of my boss, with the people I lead, or with my colleagues?"

The answer is yes: it will address all of those aspects. The Birkman was designed for people in the workplace and is sophisticated enough to capture all of those relationships as part of the many layers and hidden nuances of your personality.

"It is head and shoulders above any instrument out there because it is applicable to normal, productive human behavior, as opposed to many other assessments, which gravitate toward clinical or abnormal behavior. Everything I learned in grad school was looking at abnormal behavior," says consultant Dana Scannell of Newport Beach, California, who has a PhD in psychology. "The Birkman allows us to look at human behavior in terms of who people really are inside, as opposed to the fear of who they might be found out to be. Even when people do have things that aren't according to the norm, we say it gives us insight into understanding that person."

The Birkman will show the way you relate to those around you, your interests, your strongest points, where your comfort zone lies, and, perhaps most important, how you can recharge your energies. It helps you understand in a concrete way the conundrum that the flip side of defining your strengths is recognizing your weaknesses. As any athlete will tell you, your best attribute is also your most vulnerable point. You have to recognize when your strengths aren't being put to their best use, or they will be your undoing. If you're a tennis player or a drummer, ultimately you're going to have issues with your elbows because that's what you use the most. A boxer doesn't have to worry about laryngitis, but an opera singer does. Someone whose strength is a tireless work ethic is also the most likely to suffer burnout.

TAKE THE QUESTIONNAIRE

Now it's time to take the Birkman questionnaire, so set aside a comfortable, uninterrupted thirty to forty minutes. You can access the questionnaire at http:www.birkman.com/book. Along with your complimentary Life Style Grid Report, you can also choose to receive one of several additional topic-driven reports that are included with your purchase of this book. Select your additional free report, and then click the Start button to begin.

Have fun taking the survey: relax, and go with your first hunch on the answers. Don't try to game it. The 298-question survey is sensitive enough that it can detect unnatural answers and will reject them in the final results.

After completing and submitting the questionnaire, your report will be e-mailed to you. Please provide us with a valid e-mail address when prompted. If you need assistance with accessing the questionnaire, please complete an online form at http://support.birkman.com.

The test you are taking is the authentic Birkman assessment. Your resulting report is an abbreviated, free-of-charge version of the full Birkman feedback report. After completing the assessment, you might consider purchasing a full Birkman feedback or one of dozens of specialized formulations addressing your specific needs. The Birkman offers many different ways to see your unique information, relating it to two major categories: career and interpersonal. All such reports are derived from the original assessment that you submit. Anyone who wishes to speak with a certified Birkman consultant or who would like a full report or any one of a number of the specific feedbacks can contact Birkman International through its website (https://www.birkman.com) or by telephone (713-623-2760). The many variables and interpretations of a Birkman survey are beyond the scope of this book and best approached with experienced consultants.

The next chapter explains in detail the elements of your profile. The rest of the book then goes beyond the parameters of the free report to explain the complete, detailed Birkman analysis that has been perfected over the decades.

Remember that there is no pass or fail for the Birkman. When we say there are no wrong answers to the survey, we mean it. The Birkman is used to identify the preferences, motivations, and needs that best suit you for meaningful work. Remember too that no single test can ever capture the whole of any person's experience and wisdom. Nevertheless, going through this assessment can give you a degree of greater self-awareness and the vocabulary to express that knowledge. The Birkman aims to help you seek the best course of action to meet your inner requirements even as they change over time. Throughout the book, you will read examples of how people used the assessment to get to the bottom of a variety of problems and then applied their greater understanding of their environment to work past anger, gain a new perspective on their ordeal, and begin the dialogue and action needed to correct the situation.

YOUR BIRKMAN RESULTS

When you approach an unfamiliar park or building complex, you sometimes find at the entrance an overview map that shows you a symbol pointing to a location stating, "You are here!" You can use the Life Style Grid to get such an aerial view of yourself or your company, organization, or even family. In broad-brush terms and with a simple visual, the grid helps to define your personality and where you fit into the overall population.

The Life Style Grid is a summary report that contains these elements and the symbols that represent them:

- A four-color background that represents the landscape of society as a whole, based on the basic personality types of the general population.

- Four symbols representing your Interests (asterisk), Needs (circle), Usual Behavior (diamond), and Stress (square) as they fit on that color landscape. Needs and Stress together form one point.

- A triangle drawn from these basic pillars of the assessment, presented over the four-color graph. The exact shape is another clue to your unique personality.

Taken as a whole, your grid profile shows your interests and socialized styles based on a model of how people behave in general. In other words, it is you in relation to society as a whole. The summary can help you see your communication style, reveal whether you are task oriented or people oriented, and help you discover your unique strengths.

For consultant Tony Palmer of Atlanta, one of the most appealing aspects of the Birkman profile is the way it focuses on strategy rather than tactics in clarifying work-related goals. "Tactics are all the things you hear about," he says. "Is my résumé right? How do I network? How do I negotiate my salary? Strategy—what you want to do with your life and what you're best suited to do—that's what the Birkman answers. The biggest breakdown in career development can come when people skip the strategy piece and focus only on the tactical. They end up going to work at something just because their uncle did it or their husband or wife told them to do it."

Tony likens the process to taking a trip: "You can't pack your bag until you know where you're going. You'll pack differently for San Francisco than for Cancun. The Birkman will point a way to get to where you want to be."

And the Birkman will help to ensure that you will always find your ideal position in any organization no matter what combination of colors you might be shown to be in your report. That aim is well within your reach, because the four colors should also be thought of as representing the natural, linear process that every endeavor uses as a means to accomplish its goals. Blues start with an idea; Greens get the buy-in; Reds get it done; and Yellows keep it going by maintaining the order and the system.

THE BIRKMAN AT WORK: YOUR RIGHT PATH

The Birkman helps give people direction at various critical junctures in their careers: deciding on a field of study, getting hired, getting promotions, and the biggest midcareer hurdle: the realization after years of success that "what got me here won't get me there." It is particularly useful in bringing order to some of the more chaotic aspects of the workplace. That is because your unique Birkman feedback report builds on layers of self-awareness you may not have been able to discern yourself and suggests how to apply them to real-life situations to reduce stress and focus on what makes you productive and enjoying what you do. Professionals have a consistent need for road maps, such as when they find themselves lost in a career without a forward plan or want to find a direct route to a new position. The goal is to be prepared when an opportunity for advancement presents itself.

The Right Career

Anne Morriss was at a low point in her career, unhappy in her job at a Washington, DC, nonprofit. She had worked five years in Latin America managing public health services in rural areas, a job she had loved but saw as a stepping-stone. She had moved to Washington for a fundraising job for the nonprofit, which specialized in global development work. "I thought I was just in the wrong organization, that there was a perfect place for me in the nonprofit world, maybe not in global health, but in another bleeding-heart initiative," says Anne. "That was my self-diagnosis, but my diagnosis was way off. So I thought, 'Let's bring in the experts!'"

She was introduced to a Birkman consultant and completed the questionnaire. Anne found the message clear, concise, and provocative. "No one with this profile ends up making these choices," the consultant, Barbara Robinson, told her. "You have needs that are not being met—a need for challenge and purpose, as well as for concrete rewards and a certain amount of risk."

People with such needs, she continued, typically pick roles in highly competitive private industries. But Anne had grown up in a family of academics, lawyers, and teachers. No one had talked about the business environment as being rewarding. She had no role models in that area and so began to network to get a look at the business world. At Barbara's encouragement, she also took her GMATs and earned a master's in business administration at Harvard. After graduation, Anne started working at a for-profit company, but one with a mission. Any company she worked for, Anne says, had to have "a purpose to the entity that is bigger than making money." Such a choice would be essential for someone with such a high Interest score (90) in Social Service, Barbara adds. Eventually she joined a company helping entrepreneurs in emerging markets develop business strategies, sometimes dealing with the heads of states of those countries. It was a perfect fit. "The Birkman sped up the working process," she says. "I would have gone on the trial-and-error path, but this let me make a pivot earlier than I would have, and I'm really grateful for that."

A Hidden Talent

Consultant Cy Farmer, an international representative at Cru, a religious organization based in Germany, offered to give the Birkman to one of his daughter's high school classmates. The teenager had decided to be a nurse, but after one year at school, she returned home to tell her father: "Nursing just isn't what I expected."

Cy told her that the Birkman had her pegged as having a strong affinity for accounting. "Where did that come from?" she said, rolling her eyes, the consultant recalls. But after giving it some thought, she decided to try an accounting course, as Cy advised. She did and found it to be a perfect fit.

"She probably would have been a good nurse," Cy says, "but she would have been the nurse who kept the stats—and not feeling as fulfilled."

Many Interests, One Career

Consultants report that demand is growing significantly at the earliest stages of career planning. As tuitions at major colleges continue to soar, parents want to know that the money is going to be put to its best possible use for their child. Up to 80 percent of students entering college say they aren't sure what they want to major in, even if they have initially declared a major, and up to 50 percent change their majors at least once before graduation—some several times, according to Michael J. Leonard in the division of undergraduate studies at Pennsylvania State University.[1] And despite complaints that schools are turning into vocational education schools, far too many graduates feel they are set adrift after study.

Wendy Andreen, PhD, a Houston-based college and career counselor, says it's a mistake to spend so much effort preparing students academically for college yet so little time "to help them discover who they are—interests, personalities, potential careers—and supporting those talents." Her son plowed through four majors at the University of Texas, Austin—first in architecture, then architectural engineering, then chemical engineering. When the school's career center gave him the Birkman assessment as he was graduating, it showed him with high interests in music, science, mechanics, and literature. Just as important, it pointed to a high affinity for outdoor activity and a feeling of freedom. "Sitting behind a desk in a traditional office wasn't going to work for him," his mother says.

Michael was thrilled with the information: "It was the most objective analysis of myself that I'd seen, and I couldn't argue with it," he wrote in an e-mail to Wendy. "That was liberating, and I finally felt like I had the license to go and change my direction."

He changed his major to English with minors in math, science, and business, so he could graduate quickly. He entered the University of Texas, Dallas, and earned his master's in fine arts in what his mother calls his true calling: video game design. He was asked to stay and join the inaugural PhD program for arts and technology, specializing in game sound design.

Wendy was so impressed by the Birkman's role in helping her son that she became a Birkman consultant herself and has been working since as a counselor to college-age students.

Before the Birkman assessment, Michael had been stubborn about his choice of major, wanting to major in "something concrete." His parents, meanwhile, were trying to get him to follow his heart. "If they're fighting what they love, somewhere down the road they're going to be unhappy," says Wendy.

Wendy tells students to think of Birkman as a compass. Adults, she says, should think of it as a road map. No one wants students to stop exploring different classes or fields of work. But students will want to avoid ending up in jobs that don't suit them.

2

Identifying Your Strengths

If you know your strengths and interests—and how to keep them charged—you can play them off the assets of others and make yourself a desirable employee for any company. No matter what your Birkman results are, they will show your potential to any company looking to balance its staff with a variety of competent employees. They also will show how to improve your approach and performance in any situation.

"Look at your Birkman and be proud of it!" says Jan Brandenbarg, senior consultant in the Netherlands. "Just look at what you can do in a better way or a different way. The main thing is you learn to accept who you are. If you don't accept yourself, do you think your boss will accept you?"

THE UNIVERSAL FOUR

Your Birkman assessment begins with the Life Style Grid, which recognizes four overarching personality types that are widely acknowledged in psychology. Birkman uses them in a unique way, but didn't invent this matrix. The genesis of the idea of the universal four goes back at least as far as ancient Greece. Hippocrates declared that four types of people make up the population of the world, and this concept has endured through the centuries in various forms and terms in different cultures. It is best known in modern times in the work of Carl Jung, a pioneer in social psychology. The Birkman considers this four-part distribution to be natural in society and necessary in all organizations, and treats it as a prerequisite for the healthy functioning of the world as we know it.

The four color quadrants on the graph represent society as a whole. Your grid profile provides a broad-brush summary that gives you an overall view of where you excel. It plots your interests (averaged) and shows where your interpersonal or socialized styles fall based on a model of how people behave in general. Where your interests fall on that graph will pinpoint where you like to focus your attention and where your dominant work preferences are. Attributes are associated with each of the four colors and the general job categories they represent (figure 2.1).

Blue (Thinker/Designer)

Blue is associated with the person who inhabits the world of concepts and ideas. These are people who enjoy being creative and innovative and like to come up with fresh, even unorthodox approaches. They are reflective and tend to look inward at all possibilities. Because they are imaginative and good at connecting ideas, they gravitate to the big picture and dream of the future. They often are seen as nurturing and caring.

The color also represents art, literature, and music. Blues don't have to be professionals in these fields, but they do

Figure 2.1 The Life Style Grid

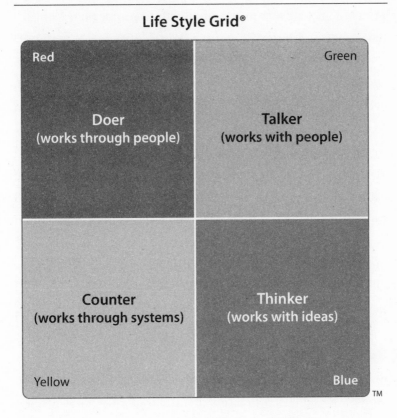

Life Style Grid®

Red	Green
Doer (works through people)	**Talker** (works with people)
Counter (works through systems)	**Thinker** (works with ideas)
Yellow	Blue

TM

consider them important in their life. In the nonartistic field, Blue can represent someone who prefers working on strategy and long-term planning. Because Blues are introspective by nature, they tend to rely on their own reactions to inform their decisions. People with Blue interests might choose careers in the fine arts, design, research, medicine, or strategy, for example.

Green (Persuader/Communicator)

Green represents people who are good communicators— persuasive people who relish being in contact with the public and are comfortable with social interaction. They are group oriented, never seem to tire of talking to people, and feel they never meet a stranger. If you say "Party!" they say, "I'm there!"

They are comfortably assertive, typically talented at selling, and are seen as having an abundance of charm and enthusiasm, even while being strongly competitive. They can be relied on to get a good understanding of people and then react instinctively to give aid and support. They tend to be more direct and assertive than their Blue brethren, and their focus is on the external world. They tend to be good at motivating others and supporting change, and the change they expect is for the better.

In a professional environment, they can channel their love of people into work in highly communicative fields, such as sales, preaching, public relations, law, politics, motivational speaking, and media.

Red (Implementer/Expediter)

Red is the color of the implementer, the hands-on doer, the builder. Reds have a practical bent and often possess a sense of urgency about getting things done. For this reason, they can excel as first responders in emergencies because they are thought of as making good, quick decisions and managing in crisis. They are pragmatic in their approach, being goal oriented and focused on the facts. They tend to be adept at technology.

They also tend to like the outdoors, where they might be employed in landscaping and building. They typically enjoy hiking, camping, and biking. An explorer might be a Red, particularly modern explorers who might need to be technically savvy as well as adventuresome. Some of the Red professions are engineering, information technology, mechanics, law enforcement, crisis management, security, construction, park ranger, and energy-related jobs, such as oil rights and petro-chemical fields.

Yellow (Administrator/Analyzer)

Yellow denotes a person who guards the system and values the numerical and the clerical. They are conscientious people who enjoy the process and procedure associated with any task. They are good at paying attention to details and are thorough in their examination. That means they represent order and seek to do things in a systematic way, insisting on checks and balances. For that reason, they also are often the ones demanding fair treatment.

On the job, they plan the work and work the plan. They don't get frustrated or bored by repetitive tasks, but instead relish the consistency. They get into the routine and maintain precedent to provide order and predictability. They don't mind doing their work calmly behind the scenes and prefer not to be interrupted when they are focused on their tasks. Yellow job titles include accountant, banker, financial analyst, controller, fiscal officer, organizer, office manager, and administrator.

ADDING COLOR

Getting a view of the color landscape of an entire workplace can reveal one of the most stubborn problems in hiring: the tendency of bosses to hire people like themselves. On the individual level, such a view can help those dominant in one color to see where to develop other aspects of their personalities. Even a superstar can't excel on all fronts and will lack qualities in certain key areas.

Raymond was a chief information officer in a business unit for a large multinational corporation. When he took the Birkman assessment, it was no surprise that he was a strong Red. His strengths were his follow-through, delivery, and strong analytical skills. He had built a reputation and progressed through the ranks because of his ability to get things done and focus on goals. He was considered an exceptional manager. But he sometimes came across to others as overly focused on the here-and-how, rigid in his style, and too mired in details. These characteristics sometimes hurt his ability to connect with others at work, and he began to feel he had to close some gaps in order to stay in a strong leadership post.

Stacy L. Sollenberger, a Georgia-based consultant, had to get the executive to see that what had brought him success wasn't necessarily what would help him maintain that success. She used the Birkman to get him to start to "talk colors." Robert saw that his strengths, while still valued in the organization, needed to be balanced with new behaviors and ways of thinking that are more in the Blue realm—strategic, long-term planning versus Red's urgent and immediate response. The Life Style Grid helped him to see the nuances of different leadership styles based on other color attributes, which he also possessed although in much less intensity.

This high-level executive was particularly coachable, but we can flex our behaviors just so far: we can't change our fundamental styles. Some leaders will find they must partner with or at least take the advice of people whose behaviors and styles are very different from their own. Executives who know how to best leverage the power of their Blue, Green, Red, and

Yellow colleagues will succeed faster and last longer in their careers. Not leveraging the different styles can cause a clash of personalities and professional styles among people who have to work closely together.

A new employee at one Houston company says that seeing his color designation and that of one of his colleagues was a revelation for him and led to a big change in how he functioned at work. "There was a woman at work that I hated," he says. "Every time I came up with an idea, she would shoot it down, saying it wasn't practical or it wouldn't work. After we did the Birkman, our consultant pointed out that I was a Blue who liked thinking about new strategies. My 'enemy' was a Yellow. I realized, then, that she wasn't out to get me after all. She was just a numbers person. It was what she felt comfortable doing and how she contributed to our office. Now, before I tell my ideas to the whole group, I run them past her to see how I might have them make better financial sense. Not only do I like her now; I feel she has helped me a lot."

The first rule of the Birkman is the one that is hardest to put into practice: how we view the world and the filters through which we perceive our environment may be very different from those of the people around us. Our standard is not *the* standard. We are not the "normal" one because there is no normal.

"Once you truly understand your perceptions and the biases and assumptions they carry, you'll be able to better manage your work and personal relationships, making both more fruitful for all involved," Dr. Birkman has said.

This personality diversity is important in the changing face of companies, which have an ever-growing variety of expertise within them. An innovative high-tech firm certainly needs a different sort of leader than a small medical facility does. In past decades, Birkman consultants tended to find a lot of assertive Reds and Greens at the heads of firms. This might be expected at a time when the biggest corporations were tied to heavy industry and many of the business leaders had been in the military. But with more diversity in the workforce now and a workplace changed by technology and other innovations in the way business is done, Birkman has found that a wide range of people representing all personality types are now in leadership positions.

PEOPLE ORIENTED VERSUS TASK ORIENTED

A number of positive-psychology assessments focus on the four-types theory; the Birkman, however, uses the grid as a foundation for building a multilayered profile.

Another dimension is added to the Life Style Grid by putting the four color quadrants in the context of two professional aspects (figure 2.2):

1. Your focus, or whether you tend to be task oriented or people oriented in how you work
2. Your work style, or whether you prefer to communicate directly with people (assertive) or indirectly (reserved)

The bottom Yellow-Blue half of the grid shows the tendency for indirect communication. The top, Red-Green, represents direct communication. The left, Red-Yellow side of the grid, is the task-oriented half, and the right, Green-Blue, is the people-oriented side.

Figure 2.2   Work Style Preferences

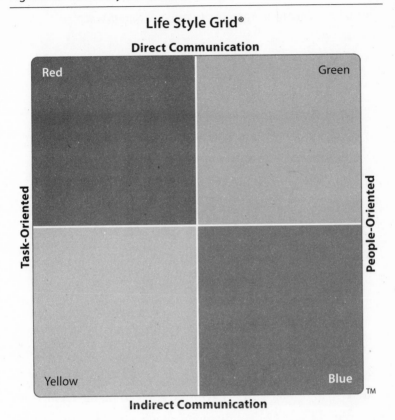

INTERPERSONAL STRENGTHS

The next step in deepening your self-awareness is to take a look at how the colors are combined to form your personality because you know instinctively that there is some of every color inside you. Locate the four symbols on the grid landscape that identify aspects of your personality. These are your interpersonal strengths—not only who you are but who you are in relation to the rest of society. They reside in the color quadrant that best represents how you express those aspects. Plotting on your Life Style Grid the analysis of your responses to the assessment questions makes your complex personality profile easier to conceptualize. The four aspects of your personality are

- *Interests*—the asterisk: WHAT you like to do, or where you gravitate in terms of your activities
- *Usual Behavior*—the diamond: HOW you like to do it (your socialized interpersonal behavior) or how you see yourself and how others will see you
- *Needs*—the circle: WHERE you ideally would like to be, that is, your expectations of the world around you and where you find your comfort zone
- *Stress*—the square: your frustrated, reactive behavior that can occur when your needs go unmet

What you are looking at is how different compartments in your life take on the attributes of a certain color. Your Interests color, for example, could be very different from the color of your Usual, or learned, behavior, which can be different from the color of the environment in which you like to work or recharge. That may sound a bit confusing at first, but our personalities are complex. Any assessment that pins a simple label on you or assigns you to one type is selling you short. Who would say that human behavior is ever one-dimensional?

Looking at the grid now, you will instantly be able to see where your energies and passions will be directed in terms of working with people and ideas, or with details and tasks.

Interests

Your Interests asterisk is in the color that best represents what appeals to you most in your life (figure 2.3). In this case shown in the diagram, the asterisk in the Yellow quadrant indicates a leaning toward the numerical and administrative side of a job. Interests are important for us to know because they say much about what satisfies us over the long haul. When an employer can connect what a person truly loves to do with that person's job, employee retention skyrockets. We like to say that whether it is an income or an outlet, your Interests keep you more happily engaged in your work and your play, and both types should be part of your daily life.

You probably know pretty well where your interests lie, and despite your feelings of growth and advancement through

Figure 2.3   The Interest Asterisk: What You Like to Do

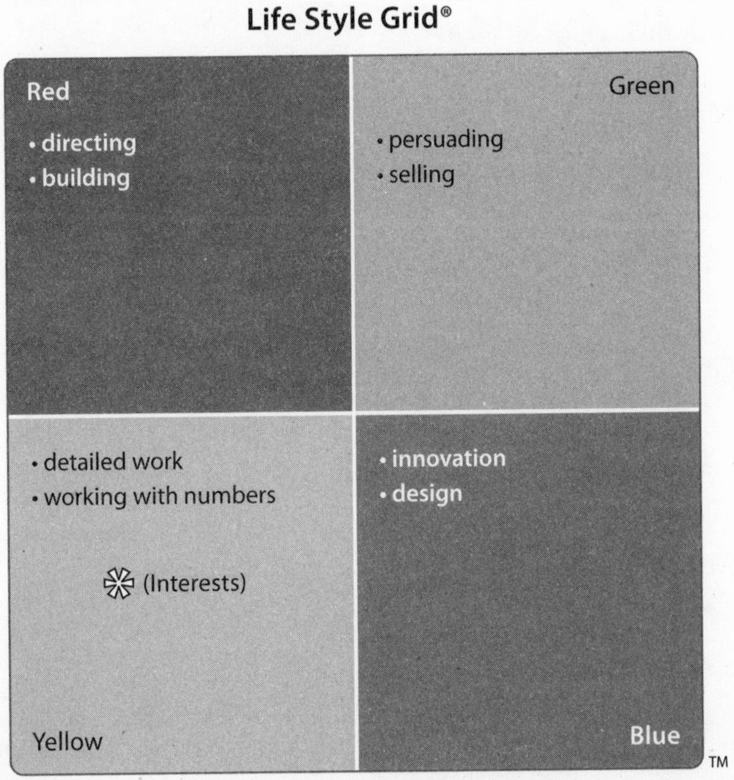

Life Style Grid®

Red	Green
• directing	• persuading
• building	• selling
• detailed work	• innovation
• working with numbers	• design
✳ (Interests)	
Yellow	Blue

TM

life, those interests have changed little since childhood. We have all heard stories about when accomplished people first discovered their passions. Biographies of violin virtuoso Joshua Bell, for example, include a story of his parents finding their four-year-old son in his room plucking out a musical tune on rubber bands he had strung across the knobs of his bedroom dresser.

Your asterisk on the Life Style Grid was derived from your average ranking on a list of ten basic Interests representing the four color fields. These are activities that you enjoy and find fulfilling. They may be tied to your work duties or as a way to recharge when you're not at work. The Areas of Interest show your natural mix of types of Interest and the degree to which they are important to you. The Areas of Interest, in connection with their color attributes, are

Blue
- Artistic
- Literary
- Musical

Green
- Social Service
- Persuasive

Red
- Mechanical
- Outdoor
- Scientific

Yellow

- Clerical

- Numerical

Your Interests aren't necessarily what you're good at; that is, they are not a measure of your skills or any innate talent. Rather, they are what you like to do or what appeals to you. You don't have to be an opera singer to be an opera buff or to play the saxophone to love jazz. But if those Interests are important to your life, they will be a source of your energy and well-being. For that reason, companies have begun to be more flexible in accommodating employees' lives outside work. It ultimately boosts productivity.

"I can't draw," Shelley Hammell, an Atlanta-based consultant, tells her clients. "If you asked me to draw a person, I'd still draw a stick figure like a kid, maybe add that little flip-do to show one is a female. I have no artistic talent. But my artistic score in the Areas of Interest is high, and I love art. If I'm on a business trip, the first thing I do after checking into a hotel is to see if there is a museum nearby. I use art to relax and to recharge."

Yet because people tend to be good at what they like to do, you may have become skilled in one of these categories. In the workplace, think of them as strong indicators of how you prefer to direct your energy, all else—pay, prestige, and opportunity—being equal. Birkman has learned that our Areas of Interests show us a nutrient in our lives—something that strengthens our emotional well-being. In addition to using the scores to point to a career path, improve your work environment, and tailor a job to suit you, they also show you what you require in your life to maintain your energy.

The ten areas, a measure of your passion for one of the fields, whether or not you make your living in it, are ranked from 1 to 99:

Under 10	Something you would prefer to delegate to others
10–39	Something you probably would rather not do if given the option
40–60	Something you can take or leave
61–75	Something that is probably a regular activity
76–90	Something you are likely to feel you can't live without
Over 90	A true passion that can turn a life around

Feeding our most vital interests is as essential to feeding the spirit of a person as water is to a plant. So a high score means it is an Interest that is likely to inform your choice of work as well as your recreation. You have to tend to your passions when you are trying to be at your creative and productive best. This is especially true when you have to work your hardest over many hours—exactly when your obligations can obscure your Interests or start to crowd out time for recharging.

You won't find it easy to turn your focus away from the task at hand, not only because of time constraints, but because Interests can be subtle, and they sometimes get buried and forgotten over the years under career, family, and other daily demands. That is what happened to a chief executive officer at a gas company in Arkansas. He was surprised when a Birkman consultant showed him an Interest score of 97 in music.

"I'll bet you have music on your office computer," said the consultant, Bob Brewer, PhD, of Oxford, Mississippi, as he pointed out the score.

"No, I don't do anything with music, though I do like music," the CEO replied.

Bob then approached the subject from a Birkman point of view: "What are people telling you about working with you?"

"That I'm cranky and hard to deal with, and hard to get along with," the executive admitted.

"This might sound crazy, but get a radio or something to play music on and keep it on during the day," Bob told him.

The chief executive thought it was an odd suggestion, coming amid the more targeted leadership and training advice he was getting, but he did it. When Bob checked back with him some weeks later, the CEO said that one small suggestion had made a huge difference in how he felt at work—and it showed: "People are coming to me now and saying, 'You're a whole lot easier to deal with,'" he said.

Bob told him, "You're feeding the passion you have."

You have learned so far in this chapter that knowing your general color attributes can help you see gaps in your professional style and strategic thinking. Such an accurate measure of your Interests will allow you to zero in on what you need to achieve workplace balance. You now know in what areas you might need to place more focus in training or in career satisfaction.

The Birkman Areas of Interests was used at one Toronto company to help an employee in a senior position who wanted to be considered for a promotion. His Birkman showed he possessed a low Persuasive but high Social Service rating. Seeing this information, Joanne Rivard, vice president of human resources for IPEX Inc., started working with him to help him learn how to better sell his ideas. It was a typical concern at the company, which makes thermoplastic piping for buildings, she says.

The company is focused on engineering and so attracts top people who tend to be dominant Red, supported by Yellow. "But we quickly found out that without Green and Blue, they wouldn't be good leaders," says Joanne, who is certified in the Birkman Method.

Her candidate for promotion, an engineer, had an 87 in Mechanical and a 71 in Scientific, as might be expected for someone who had worked on machines for his whole career. But there was one surprise: he also had a 94 Outdoor score—the sign of a true passion. Joanne sought an opening in a next-level position that would suit his need for time outdoors. She found one: a project in another province that required travel and on-site inspections.

"With a culture of promotion from within, using a tool like the Birkman is critical to development plans," she says. "It also helps with finding people who want to mentor." She says the company has a high retention rate; some 40 percent of employees have been there more than twenty years. "Before Birkman, IPEX thought of coaching as a performance improvement plan. Only those who were ready to be kicked out of the organization would get it as a last-ditch effort. What Birkman did was provide me a basis to remove my human resource hat and become an objective coach by using the Birkman language and tools I never thought of before."

Usual Behavior

The Birkman explores your Usual Behavior—so named because it describes the way we usually show up and present ourselves in our daily interactions (figure 2.4). This is your socially desirable behavior. Your Usual Behavior is always described in terms that are positive and productive.

Figure 2.4   The Usual Behavior Diamond

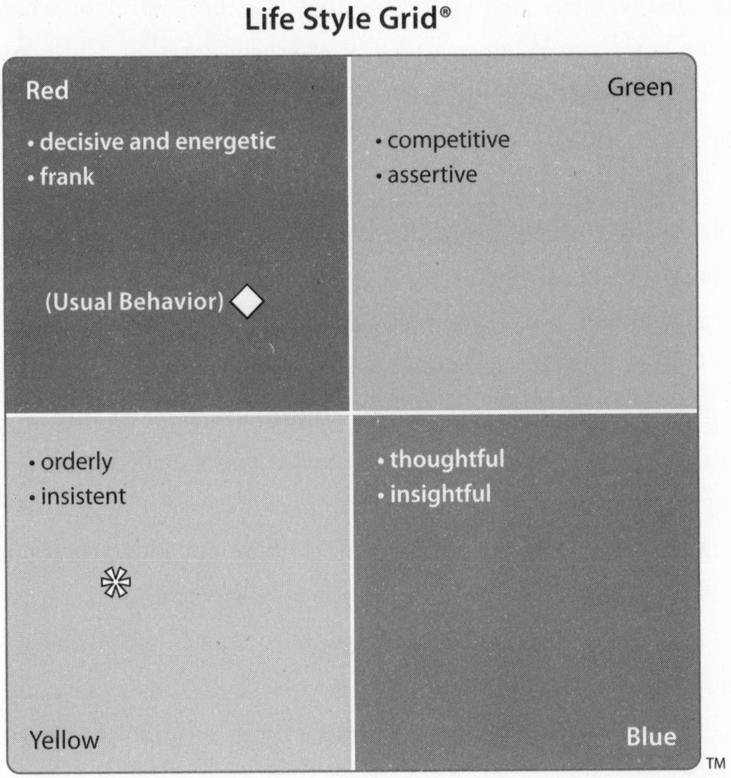

Life Style Grid®

Red	Green
• decisive and energetic • frank	• competitive • assertive
(Usual Behavior) ◇	
• orderly • insistent	• thoughtful • insightful
Yellow	Blue

TM

If your Interests represent what you want to do and your Needs are basically where you want to do it, then Usual Behavior is how you choose to do it.

In figure 2.4, the diamond in the Red quadrant suggests a person whose learned behavior is a take-charge personality.

Your Life Style Grid might show that while you have strong Interests associated with one color, you get things done in another way, with strong preferences for the environment in which you prefer to work. Some people will be concentrated in one quadrant, while others may be spread across the grid with several different colors. The grid is a simple way to view and understand at a glance the natural complexity of our behavior. There is no one way that is either better or worse than another. What matters is appreciating the depth and variety of our basic inclinations and the fascinating variety of human nature.

One information technology (IT) employee said he was pleasantly surprised to find his Interests asterisk far from his Usual Behavior marker. "I'm an IT person who loves coaching," he said, "so I was pleased my diamond (Usual) was in Yellow but my Interests (asterisk) were in Green."

Lisa Hart, a Boston-based consultant, puts an interesting twist on introducing the Birkman color grid. Before she distributed the Life Style Grid Report to a roomful of aspiring managers in one seminar in 2011, she put four posters on easels on which she had written the four colors and their attributes. She then told the participants to stand by the description that best suited them.

After the forty or so employees—most between the ages of twenty-six and thirty-three—rushed to their choices, she had a few explain what attributes drew them there. Some joked about favorite colors or colors of their favorite sports team, but an inordinate number went to the Reds, because they said it seemed to be a good leadership description.

When their actual Birkman results were handed to them, there were many surprises. One woman found she was a Blue. The person sitting next to her, whom she had known at work for some time, told her that certainly her results were wrong.

"You're definitely a Red," he told her.

"No," she replied, "this is correct. I'm a Blue. I consider myself a creative person. I was trained to be more Red, and that's the only side of me you've seen at work."

Her Birkman showed her to be a Red in her Usual Behavior but a Blue in Interests and Needs. With that information in hand, says Lisa, the woman could show her bosses that she is a better strategic planner and thinker than they might have thought. She also knows now that she has to make sure her creative Blue self is being nurtured or she'll reach a stress point. Constantly being forced to behave in a way that is against your basic tendencies causes internal struggles that no one sees but that can affect your professional performance and personal well-being.

The hope is that empowered by her Birkman, the aspiring manager will become more confident about her core strengths and better prepared to investigate the full spectrum of her personality. With her newly gained self-knowledge, she can carve out a rewarding career path, so that any future leadership role will make the best use of her biggest talents and make her work more satisfying for her and for her company.

Needs

It's trickier to discover—and for most people to articulate— what our underlying Needs are. Motivational Needs address the environment in which you prefer to dwell and how you get back your energy. In other words, they tell you what you will need to be at your best. With our Usual Behavior, we can flex or adapt our social styles as we see fit. Needs, however, remain constant. If your Needs are in the Blue quadrant, you will likely require a creative outlet to be in your comfort zone.

The Birkman gives you the vocabulary to begin a discussion about your authentic Needs. On the Life Style Grid, Needs are represented by a circle (figure 2.5).

Figure 2.5 The Needs Circle: What You Need from Others

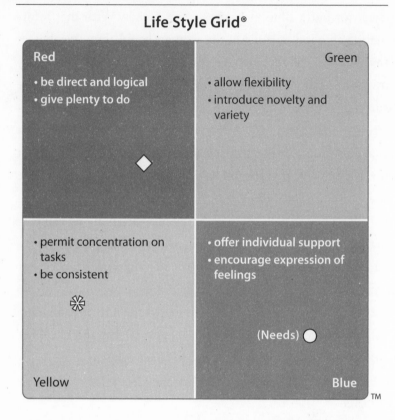

Life Style Grid®

Red	Green
• be direct and logical • give plenty to do	• allow flexibility • introduce novelty and variety
• permit concentration on tasks • be consistent	• offer individual support • encourage expression of feelings
Yellow	Blue

(Needs)

Stephan Altena of Munich works with executives across Europe and in the United States. He describes typical top-level culture as "deep Red." At a company's lower levels, they "aren't Red yet," he says, but they try to adapt their behavior as such. They conform to whatever work style is necessary to succeed, explore their interests outside the job, and tend to their personal needs away from work. It's their way of handling their work-life balance. "They say to themselves, 'My life outside work will pay me back for my efforts on the job.'"

Put another way, the Birkman can tell to what degree that person's Red behavior suits his true personality and so shows what he will need to do to get back his energy for work. "The Birkman is a good coaching tool because it's always about work and life," says Stephan. It's the only one that combines obvious behavior with behavior that isn't obvious to others, or even to the people [taking the assessment] themselves.

Stress

A critical aspect of the Birkman analysis is its ability to clarify Stress behavior. Your Stress tends to be cumulative and will manifest itself when your Needs aren't met over time. Stress is represented by a square placed over the Needs circle (figure 2.6).

Figure 2.6   The Stress Square

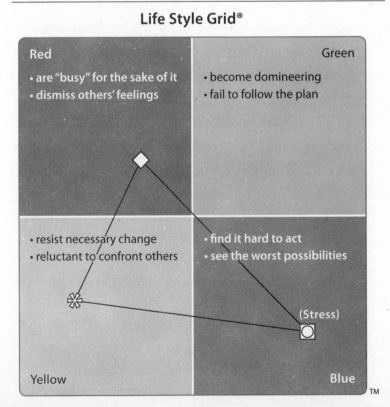

Life Style Grid®

Red

• are "busy" for the sake of it
• dismiss others' feelings

Green

• become domineering
• fail to follow the plan

• resist necessary change
• reluctant to confront others

• find it hard to act
• see the worst possibilities

(Stress)

Yellow

Blue

TM

For the most part, others can't see our deep interpersonal Needs, so we have to take responsibility for getting them met. When we fail to do this, we risk sliding into our discomfort zones—and dreaded Stress behavior. For that reason, the square in the diagram sits over the Needs circle. Just as we all have our productive strengths, we all have the flip side of our motivations as well, and that shows up as frustrated, unproductive behavior.

Stress is where many Birkman takers appreciate the relational aspect of their assessment reports. We all get frustrated at times, and we all have a bad day now and then. But although we are all prone to stress at one time or another, we don't all show it the same way.

Jonathan Michael coached a member of Parliament in Ottawa, Canada, to follow his passion outside work, based on his high literary and music Interest scores. The lawmaker had been complaining of fatigue and feeling overwhelmed—not unusual considering the huge responsibilities he was assuming. "I asked if he wrote poetry, and he lit up," Jonathan says. The politician, a Harvard-trained lawyer in the House of Commons, also was an author and, the consultant guessed from his profile, might have a poetic streak. "He said, 'When I was in Harvard I wrote poetry every week,'" but then he stopped when he became a lawyer and lawmaker.

"A lawyer should write poetry," Michael told him, and inspired the lawmaker to start writing again. He told the consultant that it has affected his life as a parliamentarian. It relieves his stress and gives him a lot of energy to go back and do what he does. "It's an act of renewal for him," Jonathan says.

The Markers Together

These four markers of asterisk, diamond, circle, and square—two of them coinciding—form a triangle whose size, shape, and general positioning hold meaning. The markers can be located anywhere on the grid, with little correlation seen between Interests and Usual Behavior. Those whose Interests and Usual Behavior are in the same quadrant might be truer to the assumed characteristics of that color and present themselves as such. They will have a certain consistency and predictability in their behavior, which could make it easier for others to read them and so meet their needs. It could also make the person a little less flexible about leaving his or her comfort zone and understanding the needs of the other types.

A wide triangle shows a broader behavioral swing with more diversity in social styles and a wide-ranging approach. The further the distance between the Usual Behavior and the Needs markers, the greater the likelihood that others will not easily see their core Needs, and the harder it will be for others to get a fix on the person's Needs. That distance also can create some confusion to others as to how to interact with them. But opposite colors also can be an advantage: other strengths might take over when needed. Whether your triangle is in one, two, or three quadrants, your strengths will be clear.

SPEAKING IN COLORS

The Birkman is one of the most-used training instruments within Wal-Mart and has particular success with team builders who are midlevel managers, says Stacey Mason, of Bentonville, Arkansas, who spent eighteen years at the company before starting her own consultancy in 2008.

The Birkman was used to address participant needs in training programs and to trouble-shoot companywide. "I'd get a call from Sam's Club or the pharmacy division asking for a way to improve teamwork or communications, or to understand how to leverage different team members within the group," she says.

Stacey spent most of her career in logistics for the company before moving into corporate training and development, where she became senior manager for leadership development. Because Wal-Mart used the Birkman, the staff were fluent in the language of Birkman colors so "there wasn't much guessing or figuring out how to navigate personal relationships," says Stacey. "People simply told you upfront how they wanted to be approached or how they preferred to get work done. They would say, 'I'm a Yellow Usual.' It was normal for them."

To explain workplace roles and how they related to the Birkman Life Style Grid, Wal-Mart's corporate-development department had some fun leading training participants in an exercise in which segments of the class were put in certain color groups and told they were going on a hypothetical road trip: taking a group of kids to Disneyland, says Stacey.

"We'd have a conversation with the people standing in each color group and talk about what they needed to take on the trip. They would talk about the trip from the perspective of their color. If you were standing in the Blue zone, you talked about how nice it is to do this for these kids and what it means in a larger context for society as a whole. Greens were riding on the bus and singing karaoke and Facebooking as we went. The Reds allowed only one bathroom break, and it had to be when we got off the interstate to get gas. And they were very clear on departure times: 'You will be on the bus at 6 each morning and when I say 6, I mean 5:30!!' The Yellows pack snacks and first-aid kits. They bring a GPS, an atlas, and a MapQuest printout, and release forms signed by parents of the kids."

THE BIRKMAN AT WORK: TEAM BUILDING

The Birkman is an effective workplace tool for building and maintaining teams from the smallest project unit to those pulled together from far-flung offices to achieve a game-changing goal. Most teams understand the task at hand, and most were chosen to be on the team because they can do their jobs well. Where teams break down is in communication and clashing ways of getting the job done. The Birkman can point out individual styles and differences and teach each team member how to take advantage of those contrasts to better reach a common goal.

Remember, the colors also represent the progression that puts an idea into practice: Blue for strategy, Green for persuading others to adopt the idea, Red for implementation, and Yellow to keep the process on track. A business needs a solid presence in all those steps. The Birkman allows business leaders to see the personality profile of their company as a whole, or any unit or team in it, and to judge whether it has the right balance to move forward.

Such a snapshot is of increasingly vital importance in the workplace, where teams often have to be formed or reconfigured quickly to meet an urgent demand. In the past, it was more common to have teams functioning together for long periods of time, allowing colleagues to form bonds and to smooth out glitches in how they worked together. Now that teams come together on short notice, it is critical that there be a way for the manager to see the big picture and for the whole staff to understand each other's contribution to the whole.

Creating Effective Team Leadership

A vice president at a Fortune 100 corporation used the Birkman to help win a multibillion-dollar government contract. The proposal submission required hundreds of employees with a broad array of skills and expertise to come together to work in teams. The company had lost the first time it submitted its proposal, but because of some technicalities, it was given a second chance.

The executive, new to the proposal effort, asked Birkman consultant Connie Charles of Delaware to help her quickly build a strong leadership team to guide the effort to win the bid. "In order to win, we're going to need to create an entirely different culture and a new way of working together," the executive said.

This vital new team—composed of people with diverse expertise in engineering, finance, supplier management, and business development—wasn't accustomed to working together. "The team came from all different parts of the company with their loyalties intact," Connie says. "Compensation, grade levels, internal processes were all different—and they weren't going to change!"

Because of the complexities of this project and its critical importance to the corporation, the consultant knew the employees would be working in a pressure-cooker environment. She counted on the Birkman's ability to anticipate how this stress would affect the team members' ability to work together. She then relied on this information to help the team avoid their stress behaviors so they could work with speed and efficiency.

When faced with such time constraints, the consultant reasoned that interpersonal relationships had to be solid. "Because of the accuracy of the Birkman data, we knew where the issues were going to come from, and then how to quickly get people to collaborate to solve them," Connie says.

"Not only did we help them build strong relationships, but we were also able to identify key blind spots in their proposal process."

Their Birkman scores, for example, suggested they would be superb team players, as their individual assessments consistently showed they tended to prefer to be rewarded as a group rather than seek individual recognition. But their idealism was causing "a competitive blind spot," Connie says. Their assumption that everyone played by the same rules and that the competitive landscape would be a level playing field caused them to overlook how their competitors were effectively tilting the playing field in their direction. As a result of this insight into the employees' motivations and perspective, Connie was able to help them identify ways to more aggressively manage the competitive elements of the proposal process.

The company completed and submitted its new proposal on time, and the team was pleased with its work. But the consultant took note of more assessment insight: the Birkman showed a strong self-critical streak in many of the team members. She knew that if they lost the bid, the team members would blame themselves for the loss. So before the outcome was even announced, Connie suggested the chief executive officer thank the proposal team so the employees could understand their hard work was genuinely appreciated. "If they lost," Connie says, "the team would have been devastated and so self-critical that no thank-you would have been heard."

But the news was good: the company won the large contract, and Connie continues to support some five hundred employees responsible for the execution of the winning program.

Starting from Scratch

Few other industries are as demanding as sports when it comes to a need to pull together a well-functioning team. Whether it is the team on the field or court, or the management team behind the scenes, athletic departments tend to be on a constant, rapidly changing cycle of building and moving.

When a National Collegiate Athletic Association Division I coach is fired or is lured to another position, it means a big move. The result is typically the termination of the contracts of everyone involved: from the person who coordinates the team videos to the director of operations, says Mary Ruth Burton of Richmond, Virginia. She is among a handful of Birkman consultants who have been asked to bring the Birkman into college and professional athletics for teams and administrators. "When a coach leaves, the athletic director has to hire a whole new coaching staff within two weeks," she says. "The speed and intensity with which this happens would make heads in corporate America spin."

The pressure is especially intense because athletic administrators know their careers depend on successful hires, especially the head coaches and their staffs. Wise athletic directors and coaches do their research and build relationships with potential candidates for these positions. But choosing the right candidate and then pulling the personalities together into a successful unit can be an organizational nightmare. It's important, Mary Ruth says, to have a coaching staff with a broad mix of work preferences and styles to deal with widely disparate demands, from the grinding pressure for consistent winning results to nurturing the young athletes.

The world of Division I college and university sports, made up of some 347 schools, is particularly volatile. Mary Ruth was executive coach to Norwood Teague who led a staff of sixty as athletic director at Virginia Commonwealth University, when he suddenly snagged a Big Ten job as athletic director at the University of Minnesota in June 2012. She helped him prepare for a much expanded leadership position in which he would oversee rebuilding a management team that was responsible for more than seven hundred student athletes. The students played for wide variety of teams, from Olympic sports to men's and women's basketball, football, and ice hockey.

"Athletics is so fast-paced and demanding," said Norwood. "We must be strategic but also make decisions quickly. Birkman is an amazing tool for getting folks in the right roles and getting a team understanding how to deliver quickly."[1]

Mary Ruth started by providing executive coaching to Norwood to help him develop strategies. She then interviewed his leadership staff, as well as a long list of people inside and outside the athletic department who had a stake in its future: staff, coaches, assistant coaches, trainers, fundraisers, faculty and the university president's office staff, and athletic department donors. She was learning about their goals and expectations for the department—"We want them to win"; "We want them to connect with us"; "We want them to develop the student athletes"—so that she could help the administrators work out a plan to achieve those various demands. She then used the Birkman to help determine what kinds of strengths were needed to implement that plan. "If they were all Red and Green, they might be good at raising money and getting results, but would they be thinking and planning enough for the future?" asks Mary Ruth. "When strengths are clear, the Birkman provides a path for the Red leader to either work on the plan or to get help."

Staff members, after all, are guiding a group of young people on the field or court with an eye to helping them in their studies as well as how to grow to be responsible adults. In that way, she thinks of coaching staffs as functioning like families. One of her concerns is to keep everyone alerted to Stress behavior. With a staff of seven hundred students from ages eighteen to twenty-one, there is anxiety on the part of the athletes about their well-being, their athletic success, and their academic performance.

The consultant also will be prepared to hire new coaches should Norwood need them. For now, she is making sure he fills vacancies with the right people in the right jobs. Mary Ruth doesn't hire individuals based on their Birkman profiles, but she uses the assessment to understand the innate strengths of candidates—statistics, logistics, motivational coaching, or creating new approaches to winning—that drew them to the work in the first place.

Once the staffers are selected, she uses the same Birkman report to get everyone "on the same page" and working together immediately. "We do team development sessions with new staffs of coaches or administrators to speed up their understanding of one another's strengths, motivational needs, and reactive behaviors," she says. "A great administration or coaching staff can figure these things out over time through trial and error, or they can get it right from the start," she says. "The Birkman is a great insurance policy for getting it right from the start."

Odd Man Out

One of the more typical problems Birkman consultants are asked to handle is when a staff has one or two members who seem to be always at odds with their colleagues, despite being qualified employees who pull their weight.

A California technology start-up was faced with this problem when they realized a member of an important team was constantly butting heads with colleagues. Betsy Cole, a Waltham, Massachusetts, consultant, sat in on a regular team meeting to see how well these creative people generated ideas. The brainstorming was impressive, and she could see they were pleased with the results. But one operations vice president seemed to be exasperated and kept repeating after each good idea, "Okay, so what are we going to do about that?"

When the team members saw their Birkman reports, they discovered the source of the rift. Most of them were Blue and so were focused on ideas. They had little patience with planning how to move anything beyond concepts and to begin executing the programs. Suddenly the role of the operations manager, a Red, who was a valued and respected employee, came into clear relief. He wasn't being dismissive of their ideas; rather, he wanted those ideas to succeed and knew their designs would stay in the room unless they let him find a practical application.

"He became more appreciated," said Betsy, who sat in on more sessions. "They started saying, 'Let's turn it over to Tim.' They saw what they were doing wrong, and they began to feel they could rely on this manager to help them go in the right direction."

Performance Reviews Perfected

Steven Foster, area manager for Redefine Hotel Management, based in the United Kingdom, uses the Birkman to give performance reviews to the ten general managers who are among the staff of 180 employees across the country.

"Before the Birkman, [the reviews] were more gauged on what we called set standards," he says. "The problem is they didn't focus on people, but on the evidence that a person *was* performing. It also had a tendency to be emotional, so the important conversations were avoided."

Those set standards, he adds, amounted to simply checking off whether a manager did a performance review every six months for his reports rather than how well those reviews were being conducted. In looking at the work of the managers themselves, the reviews tended to note only how high the customer-service scores were for the hotel being managed. "If the scores were good, we'd assume the staff was happy, which of course wasn't always the case. Now we look at the personality of the general manager and how that contributes to the scores."

UK consultant Tasneem Virani introduced the Birkman to the hotel group in June 2012 and used it to help custom-fit the company's performance reviews to key competencies for various jobs and related training. "The Birkman gives a clearer understanding of the interests that drive one's performance in different areas of their job, and in coaching the individual according to their personality needs," Tasneem says. "The Birkman always helps the manager to provide a more person-centered approach."

Steven says the Birkman breaks down the conversation in a way that helps each manager identify his or her own strengths and how those can help a group achieve its goals. "This gave us detailed insight into how to have the hard conversations that sometimes we miss or don't want to have," says Steven. "As the answers are provided by the GMs themselves, it makes it easier to talk about things."

The Birkman review report gives directions such as what to avoid or how to coach an employee to offer suggestions for optimal performance. For example, one Birkman profile, unrelated to the hotel group, includes this advice in its "Suggestions for Coaching" an employee:

- Express appreciation personally but without excessive sentiment.

- Give her special, personal attention in pressure situations.

- Apply rules and standards uniformly to get maximum cooperation.

- Allow changes to be a matter of choice where possible.

- Allow her initiative and freedom of thought and action.

"Now we can really discuss their future and their focus needs to ensure we get the best out of people," Steven says of the new approach. Because of the ease of the Birkman assessment, he says, the company plans to use the Birkman as part of its routine performance review process for general and senior managers at the hotel units.

3

The Components
Eleven Personality Markers

The Birkman addresses the vast sophistication of the human personality by looking at each individual as a puzzle. Picture a jigsaw puzzle that is a portrait of your face. No one piece of the puzzle gives us all your features, but added together, piece by piece, we begin to see a complete picture. The Birkman divides our behavioral patterns into manageable pieces that make our personalities easier to comprehend. The most critical of these pieces are the eleven relational Components.

In a full Birkman report, the responses to the assessment you took as part of this book are analyzed and your scores are placed on a spectrum for each of the Component aspects. Taken as a whole, these aspects will help you put in priority order your strongest attributes and motivations. These strengths have to be well defined and nurtured, and you have to recognize what they are and when they are not performing at their best, or your strongest talents can be your undoing.

Birkman assessment takers who pursue the full report find themselves keeping their Component results at their desks as a reference for self-management for the length of their careers.

Regardless of whether you pursue your own full Birkman Component profile, however, you will find in the following chapters useful information about how some critical parts of your personality can affect your relationships inside and outside the workplace.

The eleven Components named as relational Needs are

1. Esteem—relating one-on-one to individuals
2. Acceptance—relating to people in a group
3. Structure—systems and procedures
4. Authority—directing and controlling
5. Advantage—incentives and competition
6. Activity—preferred pace for action
7. Empathy—involvement of feeling
8. Thought—weighing action and reflection
9. Freedom—personal independence
10. Change—how you deal with it
11. Challenge—self-imposed demands

This spectrum (ranging from 1 to 99) provides a view of the overall continuum of normal socialized behavior. No single Birkman Component should be viewed in isolation. Two or more Components can combine to ramp up and intensify certain behaviors, or they may combine in such a way that they will tamp down certain tendencies. For that reason, the relational Components in this book are mostly paired by topic, although an experienced consultant knows how to analyze the interplay between all of the Components. Looking at the

Component scores we ask: Are the scores low? Are they high? Which are higher? How wide is the gap between the scores? Viewed together they give an accurate personality portrait.

We provide examples of various combinations throughout the chapters that follow. Our purpose here, however, is to give you a basic understanding of the characteristics observed and how awareness of them can make your work life easier; it is not to train you to become expert in analyzing the assessment results.

Components can be invaluable tools in hiring and promotion. They are used to match candidates' attributes to job requirements as a way to bolster, but not replace, the résumé and interview process. Is it a position that requires high activity? Would it need a deep thinker? Would it require regular communication with groups of people?

Peter Capodice of Sarasota, Florida, posed those and other questions when he was asked to help fill a top seat in the restaurant franchise industry in Tampa, Florida. He was aiming to use Components to find the best possible candidate but also to be more predictive about whom he hired. The bigger question he was considering was: Is there a way to identify someone as a likely successful choice that would stay in the position for the long term?

Retention is one of the most critical issues in business, especially in big corporations, which can spend hundreds of thousands of dollars searching for an executive and then find themselves spending the same amount again when the person doesn't work out. "In hiring, some people are great at putting on the show, but ninety days later, the show changes," Peter says. "We wanted to learn how to strip away interview behavior and drill down to see what really moves the individual."

The Components helped him to go beneath and beyond Usual Behavior that is visible to the public, to show relational Needs and work motivations. For the client, he crafted a model designed to predict and prevent hiring an incompatible candidate. If there were more than ten differences between a candidate and the job requirements, the hiring team deemed the application unworkable. Let's say the candidate is direct in communication but the job demands more indirect communication. That's difference number 1. Then it happens that the manager that the new employee would have to deal with is extroverted and the candidate is introverted. That's difference number 2. The job duties require someone who is highly organized and the applicant is spontaneous. That's difference number 3. And so on.

Some differences, of course, can be easily solved and therefore tolerated. Peter recalls one instance during work with a company in Boston in which he was comparing the chief development officer, who had a high Artistic Interest score of 91 and was a stickler for presentations that were aesthetically pleasing, with his vice president in charge of franchise sales, who was "a bullet-point kind of guy" with a mere 18 Artistic Interest. The company made it work by teaming the vice president with someone who could turn his PowerPoint "into something presentable."

For the top restaurant franchise post, Peter turned to his firm's large database of a few thousand franchise executives garnered over his years of consulting, which he used as a kind of matchmaking service between major franchises and possible candidates. He found a successful candidate, who was a highly experienced executive, he says. This person showed no significant Component differences between himself and the

Figure 3.1   The Acceptance Component

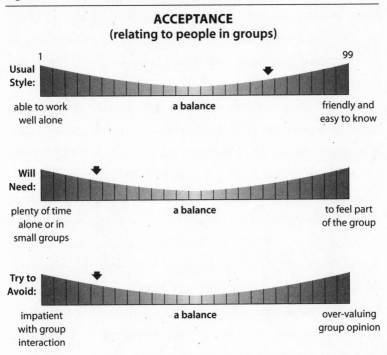

ACCEPTANCE
(relating to people in groups)

1   99

Usual
Style:

able to work   a balance   friendly and
well alone   easy to know

Will
Need:

plenty of time   a balance   to feel part
alone or in   of the group
small groups

Try to
Avoid:

impatient   a balance   over-valuing
with group   group opinion
interaction

CEO, and at most two differences with any of the four other executives on the hiring team. He also had the unique qualities of being a strategic thinker and had the ability to execute a plan—both attributes the Birkman highlighted. As of 2012, this person was doing well in his new post. "The beauty of the Birkman," says Peter, "is that it shows that people are all very different and that some can fit into a culture and give the organization what they need to learn and grow."

USUAL BEHAVIOR, NEEDS, AND STRESS

In the previous chapter, we introduced your Interests and the three basic aspects of your personality that Birkman addresses. The Life Style Grid Report presents them as an overview and an overall summary of all your responses to the assessment. Now, as we look more closely at the Components, we come back to these three important dimensions and show you in greater detail how these relational Components influence our everyday lives.

Each Component result on a full Birkman report is illustrated as a point on three bars, scored from 1 to 99, and each is equally important. One numerical score is assigned for Usual Behavior and one for Needs with its counterpart Stress. The scores are presented on three levels. The Usual Behavior and Needs scores can be thought of as working together like a pair of lenses through which we see ourselves and what we expect from others. Then the third level describes what our Stress might look like when our Needs aren't met. In this way, the Components will help you visualize the conundrum that the flip side of defining your strengths is recognizing your weaknesses. Unlike the scores for the Interest areas, these rankings are not comparative with a general landscape but instead show the intensity of the personality aspect. They signify

1–10	Extremely intense
11–39	Moderately intense
40–60	Identify with aspects of both high and low scores
61–90	Moderately intense
91–99	Extremely intense

We looked briefly at the multidimensional aspect of Birkman rankings as they related to the Life Style Grid. Here we review the three Birkman points of view as they relate to the eleven Components.

Usual Behavior

Our Usual Behavior describes how we show up to the public and interact productively in the workplace and in our daily arena. In other words, those around us can observe this behavior. It is the socialized behavior that we have learned to use to get along with others and that serves us well. This is always seen as positive in nature, because our Usual Behavior, being malleable, is the easiest way for us to adapt and modify as we navigate our days.

Needs

Others do not easily see these critical Birkman differentiators. The motivating qualities that Birkman calls Needs are unique to the Birkman among assessments, and they matter enormously. These are how we recharge and maintain our emotional equilibrium so that we stay productive. This is the reason that we begin to show signs of distress when our Needs go unmet over a period of time. Many psychological tools place people in a category of their Usual Behavior, but stop short of capturing these vitally important Needs. If we are to succeed in self-managing and cultivate a greater degree of emotional intelligence, however, we must be able to accurately identify our Needs in relation to how we interact with other people.

"If you can make sure that those closest to you understand your three most important Needs, it can be life-changing," consultant Steve Cornwell of Atlanta says. We then have to go a step further to understand the Needs of the people who matter in our world, whether they are colleague, boss, family member, or significant other. That process can be difficult. The fascinating thing about people is that in our natural diversity, we often end up having diametrically opposite Needs from those around us with whom we deal on a daily basis. Yet we have to find a way to come together and understand each other so that we can get things done and be happy in the process. Birkman can move you past the frustration to do just that.

Stress

This includes all of the counterproductive ways we act out when, over time, we don't get our Needs met. As with our Usual Behavior, our Stress behaviors are easy to see. And it isn't pretty. We don't always like to admit to this kind of behavior, but those around you will help you to understand how you look to the outside world under Stress.

Stress can be subtle but destructive. When it erupts in the workplace, it can alienate colleagues, derail teams, disrupt projects, and even sabotage a career. One major goal of the Birkman is to help you do a better job of minimizing the time you spend in Stress. By becoming aware of what happens, you can avoid getting stuck in self-defeating Stress behaviors. When you learn to recognize the early warning signs, you can quickly move away from Stress and back to productiveness. The Birkman offers in simple language what your Stress behavior will look like. It will even be able to tell you specifically—through your Component results—how your Stress behavior will look to the person you're dealing with who has a different perspective from you. This is where the Birkman comparative reports can be valuable to coworkers. "Use the Birkman Stress pages to self-coach," adds Steve. "When you are stressed, use the report to find solutions to what's bothering you." Talking to a Birkman consultant first will help to clarify the complexity that the Birkman profile reveals. But after the initial coaching sessions, most clients find it easy to refer back to the Component section of their reports and the narrative that accompanies it for self-tuning and everyday maintenance.

KEEPING POSITIVE

You can't change a leopard's spots, but you can learn how to handle the leopard. People will benefit when they leverage their attributes and stay in their productive zone. It is best for the company, but more important is that it is best for you as an individual. When you understand why you are frustrated, upset, or burned out, you can manage those pain points better and get back to the positive, productive aspects of your strengths. In Birkman language, the goal is to teach you and others how to manage the disparity between your positive outward behavior and your core recharging needs.

When the Birkman is introduced to a group that interacts with each other in the workplace or in any other setting, a new dialogue can begin that is more nurturing for each individual's needs.

An experienced consultant knows how to analyze the interplay of the thirty-three numbers that make up a complete Component report, and especially the significance of the Usual Behavior versus the Needs scores. The detail offered by the Birkman is remarkable, and the information is full of surprises, if only because most people don't have such conversations with themselves, let alone with colleagues. It reveals truths and subtleties about workplace demands and performance that might never otherwise be articulated.

Is the best boss for you the one who is personable and asks you about your family and favorite films as they stop for an occasional chat? Or would you prefer a direct, no-nonsense boss who bullet-points instructions and e-mails you a clear plan of action? The type of boss you actually prefer might not be what you would typically view as the ideal boss. Alternatively, it might also not be the authority figure any particular boss wishes to be. The Birkman will point to what best suits you in the workplace, giving valuable information about productivity and how best to communicate between boss and direct report.

Every one of the myriad combinations of factors in your personality report is going to have its advantages and disadvantages. Seen as a whole, it will describe what you need for your own self-fulfillment, how you relate to colleagues and those closest to you, and how people in your environment see you. Showing people how their individual style affects others has opened a lot of eyes in workplaces worldwide, whether the employee is dealing with reports, customers, colleagues, or bosses. The assessment feedback offers a basis for a new kind of conversation.

THE BIRKMAN AT WORK: NEGOTIATIONS

The Birkman is often used to great advantage for every sort of negotiation, where a deep understanding of the motivations and mind-set of the people across the table can greatly aid talks. At the heart of the Birkman, after all, is learning to recognize differences and then create harmony where compromise seems most difficult.

Dana Scannell of Newport Beach, California, has used the Birkman with success since the late 1990s in his role as adviser to a large union doing business with a major U.S. airline. He facilitated the negotiation of a precedent-setting four-year contract between the carrier and the union, which represented several thousand employees. He was working for the union, and so had little information on the other side. But the union members had their Birkmans in hand and had become familiar with Birkman vocabulary; Dana helped them to use their own results to understand management's thinking.

The mood in the small negotiating room at company headquarters had long turned grim over the two years that the talks dragged on, Dana recalls. There were some twenty participants, including four negotiators plus four attorneys on each side, crammed into the room, sitting around a table that formed an open square in the center of the room. Negotiations were formal, but jackets were shed at the door, so it was just shirts and ties for the mostly male group. The negotiators had grown cordial enough toward each other over the months, but the overall mood was contentious as management came under increasing pressure to stanch the damage done by the lack of a labor contract. Progress had proceeded at a snail's pace, and there was little to show for the time invested. For months an outright logjam had formed over pay rates, protection from outsourcing, staffing levels, and overtime, among other big issues.

Dana, new to the job, had to do something to help jump-start the talks and lift the spirits of the union, which had taken a beating with its persistent demands for givebacks. For more than a month, he had near-daily meetings with the team, including some marathon sessions lasting late into the night. He would fly in to meet with the team on Monday; join the meeting with the other side Tuesday, Wednesday, and Thursday; and meet again with the union team on Friday. After each of the combined sessions, Dana and the union negotiators would huddle together to hash through what happened. That schedule went into overdrive the final three weeks of the negotiations when both sides met six days a week.

Then the strategy emerged. "We looked at each individual on the labor side and asked who they were most similar to on the management side," Dana explains. "We could see who was bugging them—their opposites. So we said, 'Let's not provoke them but build a rapport.'" The old way, he says, might have been to start chatting about the person's family: "Oh, you have three kids, so do I." But the negotiators were beyond such clichés. "We went deeper to see what made them tick," he recalls, in the manner of the Birkman strategy.

The union negotiating team would pick a strong Birkman element that seemed as if it could be related to one member of the other side, such as a high Numerical Interest, and play off it during talks with language such as, "I know we have to get to the bottom line here," and, "This is where this would get us," Dana recalls.

Another person was tagged as probably being a Blue with a Component score that suggested a strong Need to see the greater good of an action and a degree of individual freedom. "We'd start by saying, 'I know you have to come up with numbers, but we have to do what's right by the people and we have to make this look like it makes sense to the both of us. What does this feel like to you? Forget we're on the opposite sides of the table. What would fit for you and be sellable for me?'"

Suddenly things started moving. Years of slogging gave way to lively debate and compromise. Within ten days, the group had an industry-leading contract hammered out that included record-setting concessions—all negotiated amid recession and painful economic realities for the company. The union had the contract that all similar unions wanted, getting more in terms of hourly rates, job protection, and retirement benefits than they had thought possible.

The CEO of the carrier walked into the room at the end and shook the negotiators' hands and said, "We have a deal." Dana had never before seen such a gesture in all his years of union work. What the CEO said next was even more of a surprise. He went up to Dana and said, "I know you're on their side, but we need to talk." He asked if the union would lend out Dana for a limited project to improve customer service. All sides agreed. The chief executive officer had figured out what had been going on, Dana says, and he was impressed by the results.

4

Your Communication Comfort Zone

Esteem and Acceptance

The Birkman starts with the two Components that best express your tendencies regarding communication, the bedrock of effective leadership and of good business in general, no matter where you are in the hierarchy. It is hard for people to develop trusting relationships without good communication skills. But even the most articulate employee or boss may come across as uncommunicative when clashing with the styles of others at work. Most people are well intentioned, but without some assistance, it's hard for them to see something from another person's perspective. In this way, an objective metric such as the Birkman can be helpful.

The assessment takes an analytical look at your communication style by measuring two Components that relate to our social styles. Birkman calls these our

- Need for Esteem (relating to individuals)
- Need for Acceptance (relating to groups)

With this pair, as with Components in general, scores will trend toward either extroverted behavior (on the Life Style Grid it is represented in the area at the top) or introverted (bottom of the grid). In terms of communication, the Component rankings for extroversion would show a low Esteem score and a high Acceptance score. Conversely, those with higher Needs for Esteem and lower Needs for group Acceptance or sociability will trend toward introversion and show up in the lower part of the Life Style Grid.

The Esteem Component can be the harder of the two to interpret, and the word itself may throw some readers because it has nothing to do with the notion of self-esteem. What it does address is how diplomatically and respectfully you prefer to deal with another person one-on-one. Other words might be *candor* or *frank directness* to describe the low scores and *careful* and *cautious sensitivity* for the high scores.

The Acceptance Component addresses overall sociability. It is Birkman's measure of your desire and tolerance for larger group gatherings. Conversely, it suggests how much alone time you need to recharge. You may show up as outgoing, gregarious, and highly entertaining in group social interaction, for example, yet you need to restore your energies by being alone or relaxing with just one or two people close to you.

Figure 4.1   The Esteem Component

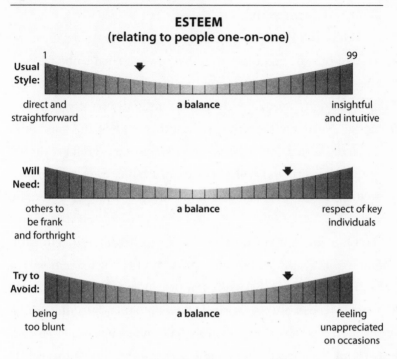

ESTEEM
(relating to people one-on-one)

Vancouver consultant Jonathan Michael has a sky-high Usual Behavior score for Acceptance of 99, coupled with a 10 ranking for Need. "I look like a people animal, but I'd rather spend alone time with my wife," he says. "I need my cabin in the woods and being by myself or with my wife."

The low Usual Behavior/high Need combination is a common Esteem score pattern (figure 4.1). It represents people who tend to be direct in their speech but prefer a response that is tactful and respectful. In other words, they can dish it out, but they can't take it. This can be a sticky combination if the person who is dishing it happens to be the boss. If a direct report abides by the Golden Rule and assumes the boss likes it back just like he gave it—frank and direct—the report may get in trouble for his candor, which the boss will likely hear as blunt and disrespectful.

Thus, the Esteem score also shows just how hard it can be to send out the right signals as to how we need to be treated. Speaking bluntly to someone may not be the best way to get that person to speak gently and tactfully to you if you have a higher Need for Esteem. At the other end of the spectrum, a person with a lower Need for Esteem may prefer a direct, candid delivery and will get uncomfortable, even a little suspicious, if the message is communicated with an especially soft sell.

One senior-level professional in health care in Houston had a typical low Usual Behavior score (31) in Esteem with a high Need score (79)—the "can dish it out, but can't take it" score. He had always worked independently, but after going through a series of promotions had ended up in charge of a team of five direct reports and working on a huge project. It was his first management post. "He was a nice guy with a good heart but very exacting," says his consultant, Phillip Weiss, also of Houston. "He continued to deliver high-quality work, but with a team, he felt he lost control over quality."

Phillip says much of his consulting work is helping executives set out on a leadership path to get "from point A to point F" at a higher position and at a higher level of functioning. The questions these executives typically ask are: "What behaviors do I have to do to get there? What behaviors will trip me up?" In this case, the executive was acting out under stress, poisoning the work climate, and tarnishing his hard-earned reputation. He would get angry and snap at his reports—behavior he had never been known for before this latest promotion. "It got really bad," Phillip remembers.

Phillip used the Birkman to look at the major categories of behavior the executive needed to consider, with a focus on communication. He told his client to think of the Birkman as an iceberg: Usual Behavior is the part we see, Needs are what are under water and so not always known, and Stress is a poke of the iceberg that sticks out of the water and becomes visible when Needs are not met.

The Birkman revealed a low-high Esteem score coupled with high Usual Behavior (74) and high Need (92) scores in Acceptance that made the health care executive feel the pressure to confront his team aggressively and in an effort to hold them to his high standards and please his senior managers.

As soon as Phillip handed his client the Birkman, the executive began to feel relief, he recalls. "It seemed to give him permission to be who he was and own it," says Phillip. "But he also knew that some of these tendencies were not helping him."

After the executive got a clear view of his behavior, he started to treat his staff better. He went so far as to apologize to several key individuals and then began to calm himself, becoming less demanding and more supportive of those who were delivering good work.

GLUED TO COLLEAGUES

Having a high Esteem Need score (90) and an equally high Acceptance Need score (90) was keeping one woman in New Jersey stuck in her job as director of information services, which she felt she had outgrown. As her Birkman scores would suggest, she had developed a strong attachment to a few of the individuals at work, as well as to her team, and she couldn't bring herself to move on. The big pharmaceutical company where she worked, however, had a culture that was completely antithetical to what she needed, which was appreciative and respectful recognition of the contributions of her and her team. The conflict was putting her in constant stress, especially because, as her Birkman also pointed out, she was very self-critical: she blamed herself for her problems and so was insisting on trying to make the job work against all odds.

The Birkman helped her see what was holding her back. "She didn't want to lose the one-on-one relationships she built in the office," says her consultant, Barbara Robinson, of Washington, "or the strong relationships she had made with her staff and her division. She also wanted to achieve the ambitious goals that she had worked hard to put in place for her staff, but the changes in the company made it clear that she would not be able to do so."

After three years of coaching, she finally came to terms with the fact that she could never change the organization to suit her needs or get it to value the goals she wanted to achieve. Instead, she landed a new job, in a more senior position at a comparable company that built on her strengths and valued her commitment to teamwork.

NO DRAMA, PLEASE

Todd Uterstaedt had a client at the opposite end of the Esteem spectrum, a manager who had been executive director at a Cincinnati, Ohio, hospital for fifteen years. She was feeling increasingly frustrated at work and had begun to break down in tears in front of her colleagues. She complained that her strengths weren't fully leveraged or appreciated, and she didn't feel she was getting adequate resources to do her job. The organization, in fact, saw her as highly competent. Her superiors wanted her to assume a greater leadership role if she could resolve what was troubling her about her job. Todd was hired to help her find what her next level of work might be.

Surprisingly, her Birkman revealed that her outbursts weren't because she was overly sensitive. In fact, the opposite was the case: she had an intense need for an emotionless and objective response from the people around her. Her high Usual Behavior score for Esteem (79), and the caring rapport with individuals that suggests, led those who had to deal with her personally to see her as diplomatic and understanding. They felt comfortable opening up to her about everything that bothered them on and off the job. Her low Needs score (9) in the same Component, however, told Todd that the executive just wanted people to do their jobs, skip the drama, and not bother her with "the messiness of all these emotions" they had been pouring out to her. Too much overt sensitivity didn't mesh with her Needs and, in fact, kept her stressed. When the manager got upset, others—as might be expected—took it as a signal that she needed to be coddled and "that just made matters a thousand times worse," says the consultant. The response pushed her to ever more emotional outbursts.

"Can't everyone just do what I tell them to do?" the director joked when she read her Birkman report. Some months later, the woman moved into a significantly more responsible position at another hospital and told Todd that the new culture was "meeting her needs" and offering her the opportunity to grow professionally. She was happy, she said, and making an impact at her new job.

NO CHIP OFF THE BLOCK

When two opposing Esteem and Acceptance profiles have to work together, they can be a good complement for the other's style, but things also can get complicated when they don't realize how different they are and how to approach the other. It can get more complicated still when the difference happens to be generational as well. Consultant Dana Scannell was called in to help a father and son in business together work out their opposite Esteem and Acceptance scores.

The business was a successful family-run real estate company in California, and the father, the head of the company, needed help with his heir apparent. The son thought of himself as a chip off the old block, but the father knew the truth: they were direct opposites.

It didn't help that they also had very different color personalities. The father was "Green, Green, Green—could sell ice to an Eskimo," Dana says. He was self-made and old school, the type who could walk into a room and have everyone laughing at his (sometimes off-color) jokes. The son was Blue—artistic and sensitive and mild mannered, and embarrassed by much of his father's patter. "He was the antithesis of what his father wanted him to be and what he [the father] was," the consultant adds.

Both father and son had similar Esteem scores on Usual Behavior and Needs and did well in one-on-one situations. However, in Acceptance, while both had high Usual Behavior scores, seeming at ease in front of groups, their underlying Needs were totally opposite, and that led to conflicts in decision making. The son, with his high Acceptance Need, felt everything he was involved in required group consensus, and the father, low in Acceptance, was annoyed with what he interpreted as his son's inability to make a decision on his own. The result was significant frustration for both of them. The problem was put in clear focus when the assessment exposed their contrasting underlying Needs. Once they understood that difference about each other, they were able to capitalize on their diverse styles, avoiding the misunderstandings that had characterized their work. By understanding and learning to appreciate their differences, they changed the tone in the office and, more important, saved their personal relationship. As a result, the father became such a fan of the assessment that he had all of his employees and candidates for jobs take it.

NOTHING PERSONAL

C-suite executives with across-the-board low sociability (Acceptance) scores were alienating their employees at one big multinational company because the bosses' behavior came across as gruff and detached. Their staff thought they didn't like them, which made the employees avoid any encounters with their bosses, creating a work atmosphere of exclusion, says consultant Philippe Jeanjean of Cambridge, Massachusetts. The consultant helped the employees see that the issue wasn't personal. It was not about them or their performance. What it *was* all about was a difference of perceptions.

SEEKING ALONE TIME

Randi Gregoire of Orlando, Florida, learned how to negotiate her Acceptance score gap of a very high 99 in Usual Behavior and a low 11 Need, meaning that although she seems to be sociable and happy to be in large groups, she needs some significant time alone to recharge. "I show up as an extrovert, very friendly," she says. "I go into a room and seek out the strangers and try to get to know them. But in my heart of hearts, I am an introvert."

When she was working in East Asia, leading an English-language workshop, she always asked to have a room to herself, no matter what the cost. "I learned that if I wanted to be able to be with people all day, teaching and leading a team, then I had to retreat at night to regroup and reenergize," she says. "I always knew that this was true about myself, but the Birkman explained why."

It's often hard for others to understand. In the evenings after work, when her colleagues began to socialize and play games, she would tell them she had to go home. "Why are you leaving?" they would always ask, perplexed. It worked the same way at home. Once her husband was preparing to go on a business trip, but at the last minute came home from the office and announced it had been cancelled. She couldn't hide her disappointment and told him she had been counting on alone time. He told her: "I'll go to the office and you can stay home and be alone."

"He knows my score, so he didn't take it personally," she says, laughing.

To complicate the issue of a high Usual Behavior score with a low Need Acceptance score is the fact that many of the people with these profiles still want to be invited to join the party—even if they are choosing not to go—and sometimes push themselves to maintain their reputations as being outgoing. Because he was so gregarious at work, one Birkman client said he constantly got invited by his colleagues to go out after hours. He would tell everyone that he was going, but then he wouldn't show up, says consultant Janice Bergstresser of Coatesville, Pennsylvania. "He actually wanted to be invited," she adds, "but at the end of the day, he just wanted alone time. The Birkman showed his colleagues that he wasn't being two-faced or difficult and that he wasn't mad at them. It was just his personality."

THE BIRKMAN AT WORK: COUPLES COUNSELING

The connection between our relationships at work and the ones we maintain outside the office is a strong one because we tend to repeat the same patterns of engagement with others. It isn't unusual for Birkman takers to ask for the assessment to be given to their spouse and the rest of the family. Similarly, therapists of all types, from marriage counselors to life coaches, are making use of instruments like the Birkman Method. They see these as reliable in assessing a conflict and understanding the individuals involved, who are otherwise simply asked to self-diagnose their issues.

The Birkman has been used for work with couples since the 1960s, when Roger Birkman held small group sessions he called discovery groups for the First Methodist Church in Houston. The Birkman is not recommended for counseling troubled marriages, but it has been used by dating, engaged, and married couples to help them see potential trouble spots and "to make good marriages better," says consultant Bob Bolling of Houston.

Bob started couples coaching in 2007 when Chapelwood United Methodist Church in Houston allowed him to offer it to the congregation. Some forty couples signed up when the minister announced it. The consultant believes the assessments can work best for people married five to ten years. After that, he says, children and accelerated careers tend to make marital issues all about a lack of time, which also means there is little room to work on the marriage itself.

Bob finds that the Esteem Component often "is the biggie" in such counseling. If both people are low Usual Behavior and high Need in Esteem, they are going to be very frank in their speech to one another, yet each of them wants to be handled more gently. And although the Birkman doesn't endorse anyone identifying a gender-specific trait, it's safe to say that, anecdotally, many male clients have been overjoyed to have such Esteem scores explained. "If he says, 'I don't like that dress,' and she says, 'I don't care,' guess who gets their feelings hurt?" Bob asks.

Karyl White went through couples coaching with her boyfriend, Charles. They both had been married before and went to Bob to see what they could learn about building a successful relationship. She had taken the Birkman twice at work but said she didn't really appreciate the breadth of the report until she took Bob's six-week couples course. "It was fabulous for us, and it really accelerated our relationship," she says, adding that they were married shortly afterward. "By having the results charted against each other, it took all the emotion out of the differences in our personalities." Their sociability scores showed clearly Karyl's tendency to be extroverted, while Charles is an introvert. Karyl's Esteem scores are 6 Usual Behavior and 6 Need, while Charles's are 21 Usual Behavior and 94 Need. Acceptance scores are also the opposite: Karyl is 98 Usual Behavior and 92 Need. Charles is 17 Usual Behavior and 17 Need.

With such high Acceptance scores, Karyl learned that not being able to interact with others could trigger Stress behavior, where she finds herself becoming overly sensitive. She even nicknamed her stressed-out personality: "'Karyl Ann,' which is what my mother called me when she was mad at me," she says with a laugh. To avoid the stress, Karyl and Charles have agreed to plan one fun social event that involves other people over the weekend. Otherwise she socializes during the week. Her husband lets her know when he feels their social schedule is getting too full. "I respect his need for alone time because it is so obvious how much it revives him," she says.

A Couple Once More

The Birkman also helps couples move into the phase of their lives where they are just a couple again, Bob says. Edward and Suzanne A. Davis were married thirty-seven years with grown children when they joined the consultant's couples circle. Bob's first impression of the two was that "they are polar opposites" because she was so extroverted and he was introverted—but their Birkman showed them to be very similar.

For both of them, the Birkman showed a high Outdoor Interest score. That was no surprise, but its importance as a way for them to recharge and restore themselves was. It came just as they were considering a possible second home. "So it gave us the confidence to buy a place along a river surrounded by nature and near our grandchild," Suzanne says.

For many couples, discovering their partner's likes and dislikes comes as a surprise. "You'd think after a number of years together, people would know their partner's Interests," Bob says. "I tell couples to guess the highest two and lowest two Interests off the Birkman list. I can count on one hand among hundreds of couples the number who got that right."

And you might think the partner with the higher Numerical and Clerical ratings would handle the money, but that's not true, Bob adds. "I often find couples determine whether the husband or wife does it because of their work schedules or something like that." He then laments, "And doing the wrong tasks is always stressful in a marriage."

Season of Happiness

Bob and Carleen Woods also were married thirty-seven years and joined Bob's group in part, they say, "to erase the stigma" that entering counseling means a marriage is in trouble. "We tend to learn about family and careers, but marriage is something we don't study," says Carleen. "We are retired, and we thought if we're in this season of our lives and if we're not intentional about what the time will look like, we could be headed for something other than a season of happiness."

Both agreed that the sessions helped them become more respectful of each other and each other's wishes. The consultant says possibly the most valuable lesson couples learn is the simple fact that their spouses are different from them in many ways and that those differences don't matter when understood.

It's the Thought That Counts

Ron Baker, a senior Birkman consultant for the Western Ontario District Pentecostal Assemblies of Canada, finds that no matter how long a couple has been married, they can often misinterpret the motivation behind routine behavior. "I had a couple who wanted to get to know each other after being married for more than twenty years," he says with a laugh. "After I did the ninety-minute debriefing, she said [to her husband], 'You know, for the past seventeen years I thought you were being a jerk. Now I know it's just your personality!'"

When individuals understand the other's uniqueness, he says, they can compensate for these differences and even enjoy the humorous side to them.

5

The Power of Process

Structure

The odd couple is a cultural chestnut: one partner is fastidious and methodical and the other, while not necessarily messy, is freewheeling and less rigid in organization. At work, the gap in styles can seem serious, with one employee adhering strictly to process and making a list of measured steps toward a goal, while a colleague prefers heart-racing sprints to deadlines.

Is one way superior? Does the methodical march to the finish line guarantee more detail and accuracy, or does working fast sharpen focus and eliminate waste? The Birkman, as always, believes there is value in everyone's preference, no matter where they fall on the spectrum it measures as Structure.

The person scoring high in Structure brings to the table a calm and orderly working environment. This relational Component was once labeled Insistence because the high scorers on this trait insist on following systems and procedures. These employees tend to say, "I'm organized, and I'll get this done my way." They often earn praise for creating order out of chaos. But don't assume they appreciate Structure for the sake of Structure or accept your idea of Structure. Many high Structure employees would rather work under their own system than be pushed to adjust to a Structure already in place. And because these high scorers are so good at putting plans in place and following through with them in a consistent and organized fashion, Structure serves as a kind of enforcement ability. It is another way to exert authority. High Structure people might be the insistent accountant who complains about your late expense-report receipts—which you feel you have absolutely no time to do.

As with the other Components, the Birkman can find value on either end of the spectrum. Components possess inherent strengths, needs, and stressors. They just play out differently depending on your score. Considerable strengths accompany low Structure qualities as well as high Structure ones.

Low Structure people bring flexibility, spontaneity, and an ability to improvise and quickly shift course. Often they are creative and function best—even thrive—when they have a great deal of freedom and elasticity in the way they do their job. Because many C-level executives are low Structure, they need staffers who have high Structure scores to help them stay organized, maintain their systems, and get things done.

Not craving Structure doesn't mean people are disorganized. They may have their own perception of being organized. They just don't need a rigid environment to do their best, and they don't want one. They also are the types who might think rules are made to be broken. Healthy organizations balance flexibility with procedure to suit both styles of Structure employees, creating an atmosphere that is organized enough to give a sense of security without stifling anyone's way of being productive. Executives have to make sure their company or organization can accommodate the variety of talent working in it. This is especially important when jobs and whole industries are going through major transformations.

STEPPING ASIDE

A senior executive at a university health center in Salt Lake City had to learn how to rein in some of her high Structure proclivities in order to get out of the way of her reports. Utah consultant Patricia A. Russell's client was a high-ranking executive who paid close attention to detail, and that meticulous way of working allowed her to build a strong career in the medical field. She climbed up the ladder at the hospital, where she was considered a conscientious and dedicated leader. She set lofty goals for herself and her team, and felt she was helping the team members achieve those goals by organizing their work in great detail, including to-do lists and thorough verbal instructions.

Invariably she was frustrated by what she saw as her reports' lack of initiative and their failure to be creative. The employees, for their part, felt that they were micromanaged and that any creative spark they had was immediately doused by directives. "Frustrated" is how they described themselves. They weren't given the freedom or encouragement to find their own solutions to problems or discover innovative ways to achieve the set goals. As individuals, each felt unappreciated and disrespected. No one could figure out why the goals, clearly within their capabilities, were being missed. And the situation didn't improve even when they started working harder.

The dynamics of the Structure Component that Patricia explained to the executive and her team was a revelation to them. The boss understood that despite her good intentions, her high score for Structure Usual Behavior, coupled with her very high Structure Need, showed how her overattention to detail stifled her team. In light of this discovery, she began to give her reports the breathing room they needed to do their best.

The boss still set goals for them, but she stopped dictating exactly how they were to be achieved. When she relaxed the reins a bit and started trusting the creative energy of her team members, they began to flourish. They worked together to meet their goals using their own ideas and initiative. So dramatic was the improvement that the chief executive reported it had an immediate impact on the bottom line: a 6 percent group improvement in revenue over several months and a 5 percent increase on average in employee satisfaction, according to the consultant. That is the power of Structure—at both ends of the spectrum.

DETAILS, DETAILS

Bob Brewer of Oxford, Mississippi, also counseled a chief executive with Structure issues. This executive had atypical scores in relation to Need and Usual Behavior, a so-called reversal. The CEO's profile showed he tended to think in more detail than he communicated. The CEO knew precisely what he wanted his staff to do and always thought that he spelled it out. But in fact he thought about things so much that when he got ready to present them, he'd give them a once-over lightly, assuming too much knowledge on the part of the others.

When he would say later, "I told you how to do this," they'd reply, "No, you didn't."

"He was forever amazed when the staff brought back something different from what, in his mind, he had asked for," says Bob. The situation improved almost immediately when the consultant developed simple feedback tools to ensure clarity and completeness. He gave them a simple dialogue as a pattern. Before they left the boss's office, the boss would ask one question: "What did I just tell you to do?" The staff would then tell him what they understood the assignment to be. They then corrected any misunderstanding.

"It took them five minutes to learn how to do that once they knew the problem," Bob says. "That engendered considerably more peace in the relationship and more efficiency in their work together."

MESSY COMPROMISE

Opposing Structure scores come up frequently in couples counseling. "I bet it's close to 70 percent of the time a low Structure will marry a high Structure," says Bob Bolling of Houston. "Perhaps it's because they admire [the traits they don't have] in another person."

Bob resolved the odd-couple conundrum with his own wife with one agreement: all of the so-called public rooms in their home are to be kept at the high Structure standards of his wife. His office is sacred ground to him, and he gets to keep it however he likes. "She closes the door when people come over," he says.

The issue of clashing Structure styles isn't as easily compartmentalized in the workplace. The bigger issue isn't any one score but how scores interact. Consultant Steve Cornwell of

Atlanta counseled Shannon Woolard when she was hired as the director for Summit Management Corporation, also in Atlanta, which owns and manages a portfolio of hotels throughout the southeast United States. She was responsible for the performance of the company's sales team and from the start wanted to optimize their work. Of the six members of her sales team, one didn't seem to want to follow procedure. The woman got all her work done, but she wasn't diligent about the paperwork required of all the reports. That lack of conformity was throwing a wrench in the overall process and was beginning to hurt her reputation among her colleagues. After the team members took the Birkman, however, they saw that she was the only employee on the staff who did not have a high Structure score.

"They all thought she wasn't a team player, but it was just that she had to do it another way," Steve says. "She was very relieved that everyone understood that about her, and afterward they looked at her differently."

"The Birkman Method allowed everyone to get to know one another in a very in-depth way," says Shannon.[1] "We still have conflict, and the Birkman provides insight into how to guide us to quicker resolutions in an environment that is about reinforcing positive behavior verses focusing on what someone did wrong."

Steve also helped a new executive with Structure issues. Jonathan Kupersmith opted for monthly coaching sessions when he was promoted to president of B2T Training in Alpharetta, Georgia. He wanted to avoid any missteps as a new leader. But before Steve could address those issues, he had to figure out how best to coach this new client. Jonathan had very low Structure scores, and Steve knew he had to tread lightly, especially not giving him a to-do list after every coaching session, his usual way of working. "I'm very high Structure and would have intimidated him if I did what I wanted to," says Steve.

Instead, they kept sessions free flowing. Each session ended with Jonathan telling the consultant what he wanted to accomplish before the next session. "This way I wasn't imposing tasks and structure on him that would have otherwise put him in stress and set the stage for an unsuccessful coaching experience," says Steve.

Steve focused on helping Jonathan align his strengths with his job. It was clear that because of his low Structure personality, he needed to surround himself with administrative-support people who could carry out his ideas and keep order in his daily workday. He also wanted to make sure that the work his reports did fit their own strengths "instead of what they think the company needs," Steve says. "That means figuring out what they need for success to reach their personal goals as well as the company's goals."

Low Structure employees seem to find their own paths to success no matter how much their process comes under fire. And their process often draws fire. Robert Hudson of Louisville, Kentucky, worked for two decades as a successful district manager for Burger King in New York and Miami, and for PepsiCo in Philadelphia. He says he always felt he was working in a style different from most other people in his workplace, especially because of his proclivity to ignore protocol and refuse to go through direct line communication. "Even getting good results, I wasn't seen as politically correct," he says. "Some in the upper echelon didn't like the concept of doing anything it takes—from landscaping to remodeling to unconventional promotions—to expand my restaurant franchises."

When someone suggested he take the Birkman, he found out exactly how his preferred style of working clashed with that of his colleagues. His Birkman showed he had a low Structure combination, with scores of 16 for Usual Behavior and 29 for Need. "It is hard for a person like me to fit into a corporation," he says. "I found it difficult to balance my disregard for the rules with my desire to get results and find innovations to improve the business."

Eventually he quit the food business and went into business for himself. Today he owns M&H Marketing, a Louisville, Kentucky, consulting firm that helps medical practices expand revenue. "I can maintain a flexible and responsive schedule," he says. "I surround myself with detail people so they can do that work for me, and I can concentrate on exploring new ideas and options. I like working outside the chain of command!"

FOOD FOR THOUGHT

Structure can have a big impact on how a team functions and clears a path to success. Wilson Wong of Atlanta recalls when he was asked to help a media company with a team that wasn't performing well. He gave a Birkman to the twelve team members and saw that their varied Need for Structure scores was an issue.

The several who had low Structure scores in their Usual Behavior were keeping busy but had no direction from their team leader, who also was low Structure. "Everyone was doing their own thing, and nothing was getting done. They didn't have any routine structure as a group, and they had high Activity scores with high Change scores, so they started on things immediately and with lots of energy—and would shift gears a lot."

The team leader had an Authority profile that showed a particular kind of boss whom Wilson recognized: "They say, 'Bring me a rock, any rock; no, not that one; no, not that one; I don't know what I want, but I'll know it when I see it.'"

To make it clear to the teammates what the source of their dysfunction was, Wilson had them do one of his "food for thought" exercises where teams prepare a multiple-course meal together and he observes how they handle it. He gave each of the twelve team members a menu for a four-course meal and also gave them a deadline. Then he sat back and watched. As expected, they split up and went in all different directions, with little discussion among them. The only planning the leader did was to get the table set. As it got close to deadline, they started turning to shortcuts. When it came time to start serving the meal, one dish was put on the table before the rest were ready, and it was cold by the time the other dishes arrived.

"It happened even though I warned them it would," Wilson says. "It was one of the worst meals I ever had."

Afterward they discussed how their Structure scores had played into the problem. In particular, he told the leader that he had broad ideas but no organization, no suggestions, and no coordination, which created overlap and lots of gaps.

A year later, Wilson led another team-building session with the group and asked them to cook a more difficult meal. This time they talked and planned before they started to cook. The team leader had a clipboard with a time line and assignments for each participant. The work was well paced, and the leader, clipboard in hand, kept control over every step. The resulting meal, Wilson reports, was delicious. The culture of the unit changed so profoundly, the consultant says, that when he checked in on the team leader two years later, his team was still functioning well despite some turnover.

THE BIRKMAN AT WORK: CORPORATE TRANSITIONS

Orchestrating Change

When a couple nearing retirement, Tom and Carolyn Porter, brought a young couple, Richard ("Jeff") and Amelia Jeffers, into their prestigious fine-arts auction house in central Ohio, a generation gap was threatening to bog down the transition. The Porters had joined Garth's Auctions in 1967 when the original owner wanted to take the thirteen-year-old company, then specializing in antique auctions, to the next level. Over the next two decades, the Porters helped the business gain a national reputation. By the mid-1990s, they began to think about a further expansion and, for the longer term, an exit strategy. They entered a partnership agreement with Jeff and Amelia after the company had grown to about thirteen employees. "It was going to be a huge transition," said Amelia. The original owner had died in 1973, so the Porters had been independent for twenty-three years. "There were issues involving roles and decision making."

The young couple joined in overseeing the day-to-day operations, but it was tough going. No one knew what roles to play in the new concern, deciding that in fairness, everyone was going to participate in every decision. But this system slowed progress. Amelia heard about the Birkman from one of the Porters' daughters, herself a certified Birkman consultant. They decided to ask consultant Celia Crossley in Columbus, Ohio, for help. Amelia's question for Celia: "How do we use our time, talent, and treasure in the company to ensure we have equal ownership and decision-making roles?"

"They kept saying that it was the age difference," Celia recalls, because the owners were in their sixties and the new couple in their twenties. "They were different, but it wasn't age."

The consultant helped them see just how tangled the relationships were: "It complicated the partnership that we had four distinct independent entrepreneurial personalities and two sets of married couples," says Amelia. "So it wasn't only the partnership—our marriage partners also were our business partners."

The four took the Birkman assessment and waited for the results. Each got individual reports, but to bring the group dynamics into sharp focus, Celia included group Life Style Grids that plotted their Usual Behavior styles, their Interests, and their Needs and Stress behavior. The good news was in plain sight: each of the four had clear strengths that were different from the others (figure 5.1).

Jeff Jeffers was the only one with his Interest asterisk in Yellow, so he was tagged to act as chief financial officer. Carolyn Porter showed high Structure scores and a strong Scientific Interest, so she did the research. Tom, with a Persuasive score of 75, took on sales. Amelia, a Blue, used her creative talents to help develop new marketing strategies and groupings of collections for sale.

The Birkman also flagged some Stress points. Jeff's results showed he was able to help plan a course of action with the group, but afterward would likely prefer to go into his office to work alone. Amelia learned she had to modify her behavior and communications style to be more patient and accepting of others' work habits.

Figure 5.1   The Birkman Tracked Each Employee's Main Interest

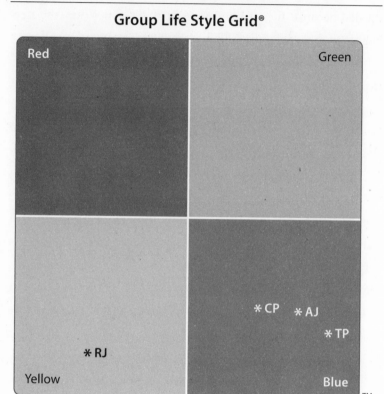

Amelia and Jeff took their reports with them as they headed out of town. She drove while he read the report. "Ah, it says you're a little dictator," she remembers her husband saying with a laugh. Her Esteem scores for one-on-one communication were relatively low (Usual Behavior, 28; Need, 49) and her Authority was the highest of the four: 66.

Amelia admits: "I don't like to be sold on something. I want the facts: 'Here's what I'm offering, no beating around the bush.' I put that out there, and it's not always good, but it's not mean or malicious."

Carolyn and Jeff both needed to have people speak gently and respectfully to them before delivering any news. The couples, it turns out, weren't pitted against each other. If there was any divide, it was Tom and Amelia on one side and Jeff and Carolyn on the other.

"Tom and I were quick to make decisions," Amelia offers as one example on the Birkman profiles. "Jeff and Carolyn needed time to think. The Birkman opened my eyes not only to what I could contribute to my business relations with my three business partners, but it allowed me to look at my marriage and say, 'Here's what I'm putting out and what I'm expecting back.'"

One area in which they were all similar and in sync was in Structure, showing high Usual Behavior scores ranging from Carolyn's 61 to Tom's 90, with both Amelia and Jeff at 79. Their Needs in the Component were all relatively low—including Amelia's rock-bottom 5. "All appeared fairly organized and planful," says Celia. "None of them needed direction and preferred to follow their own course of action. As long as they each had their respective responsibilities and followed what they felt was the correct path while keeping flexible for changes, it worked." They did that, and it did work. Today Garth's Auctions has all its new employees take the Birkman. It isn't used to filter candidates, Amelia says, but it saves time in helping new employees get placed in the company once they are hired. Most people, she says, can't bring themselves to say to a new boss: "This is what I need you to give me for me to get my job done." But that is just what the auction house management wants to hear—and what other bosses need to hear.

Amelia feels the Birkman made all the routine work in her company more diplomatic and more democratic. For example, although she owns the company, she shares an office so her bookkeeper can have her own space. The Birkman showed that the accountant needed it to focus (low Acceptance scores suggesting a need for time alone and very low need for Change).

In January 2006, the Jefferses took full ownership of the company. "We lost zero employees" during transition into sole ownership, Amelia says proudly. "I think the Birkman is a huge factor. You can't overstate how the self-awareness made us better managers." As of 2013, Garth's Auctions has a large presence in the United States and a budding one internationally.

"The bottom line," says Celia, "is that once they all recognized their behavior differences, and the 'why,' they could successfully move the business forward because they shared the same vision, hopes and dreams."

Hire Variety

The Birkman helped guide a U.K. search-engine-optimization company through a whipsaw series of transitions from 2005 to 2010: a rapid expansion from 20 to 275 employees, its purchase by a U.S. concern, and the subsequent restructuring of its senior management team.

When the eight-year-old company began its accelerated growth in 2005, riding an explosion in online-search marketing, management wasn't sure where to begin hiring. They knew they needed people at every level, especially to lead design, sales, and project implementation. And they aimed to create a competent and nurturing atmosphere for the new talent that would be coming on board.

Before recruitment began, they wanted to take an objective look at what strengths they had and what they lacked. Barbara Robinson, who was working in the United Kingdom at the time, gave nine members of the senior management team Birkman assessments. When the team saw the results, they laughed: every one of them was in the far right-hand corner of the Blue quadrant, maybe with some Green sprinkled in, pointing to the strong, creative talent that made them a hot start-up. "They immediately got the picture," she says. "The founder kept hiring people like himself!"

That one simple and very typical mistake upper management makes is at the core of many corporate woes—from a stubborn lack of diversity in company hierarchies to the kind of stagnant thinking that threatens to sink a business. The one-hire-fits-all mentality is hard to recognize amid a staff of people who tend to understand each other and get along. It can be even harder to correct.

The discussion that followed led them to begin looking first for a chief financial officer. Barbara helped them find a talented candidate who brought to the office some Yellow—a passion for accounting along with a systematic approach to the work. The new employee also had a lot of Blue in her profile, so she could find common ground with her senior management colleagues.

The purchase by the U.S. company allowed a wider expansion, and the recruitment process eventually resulted in a staff of 275. Once the new owners were in place, the founder, who was chief executive officer, left the company, and Barbara worked with the new CEO to reshape the senior-management team.

6

Are You a Boss or Just Bossy?

Authority

What does a good leader or CEO look like on a Birkman? There is no one answer. Because of the complexity of people and workplaces, a wide variety of leadership styles will suit many types of organizations and the many types of work that have to be done. No formula exists that can predict leadership success. You can lead from any combination of traits.

At best, we can find some common denominators that will suit a particular industry or organization—or at least the task at hand. More important than trying to predict successful leadership, the Birkman will show the type of leader you are and what you can do to become a more effective boss. Everyone exercises authority in several ways, and the Birkman can measure that in specific terms.

Overall, the Authority Component gives a leader a sense of how a higher or lower dominance style will be received by those being led. It answers questions about why a person may either accept or resist the way he or she receives messages from a boss. As with other Birkman Components, knowing this natural difference of command style can remove personal blame and diffuse defensiveness in a working relationship. Authority is about verbal dominance: speaking up, speaking out, arguing, liking to debate, being comfortable saying, "I told you to be here at 8:00. Where are you?" In short, the relational Component showing Need for Authority tells the degree to which people like to assert themselves by being verbally commanding.

High Authority leadership is choosing to lead people in a more overtly authoritarian way. These bosses are not necessarily barking commands, but the volume of their orders can be ramped up in a person who is also high Empathy, meaning that he or she tends to be expressive anyway. These people are typically described as more "in your face," because they are comfortable giving orders in a forceful way. They do well in roles that involve immediacy and risk, such as construction crews, factories, emergency workers, and, as you might expect, the military.

Still, the stereotype of the authoritarian boss doesn't hold sway anymore as the workforce becomes more diverse, more skilled, better educated, and well informed. An effective boss stays focused and in control but does not dominate employees. In popular culture, the "whisperer" phenomenon suggests that the best path to authority over man or beast is to see yourself through the eyes of the ones you wish to lead, forming a nonthreatening relationship that is ultimately more effective. In Birkman terms, such a leadership type is called a low Authority style. These leaders let others know who the boss is without being bossy.

THE CHANGING FACE OF AUTHORITY

After nearly twenty years as a management consultant to many chief executives in big companies, Esther S. Powers, PhD, of Greater Atlanta can speak from experience about generational changes in leadership styles, as revealed by the Birkman. When she started coaching in large, heavy-industry companies, "the leaders were like military: they were Red, high Authority, high Structure, high Activity, low Thought, low Advantage, low Empathy," she recalls. "They were the traditional managers in the plants. They didn't listen much and they were not collaborative." These high Authority executives were commanding leaders and tended to be good speakers, but they often lacked diplomacy and weren't at all welcoming to the changes that were coming as a result of competition, participatory management, and the explosion in high-tech entrepreneurship and information, Esther says. In the early 1990s, companies were starting to create high-performance work teams in an effort to become nimbler. She was brought in to do organizational redesigns at traditional manufacturing companies that wanted to stay abreast of the changes, some wishing to emulate Japanese manufacturing techniques. It was the start of the just-in-time way of doing business, with low inventories and flatter hierarchies.

"It took just a touch for me to win over people on the floor, but the managers wanted to prove everyone wrong," Esther says. "The managers would try to get me out of there."

But the economic transformation couldn't be slowed, let alone stopped. Once the new models were created, however, Esther found many of the senior managers couldn't lead the new businesses. By the next decade, she says, the chief executives were "altogether different." She started noticing more Birkman profiles of people who appeared more flexible and optimistic. She also found more Green and Blue types, as leadership increasingly demanded a more democratic and more creative touch. The old-style authoritarian leaders still exist, of course, but they are fewer in number and must share room at the top with a wide variety of people. The precision with which the Birkman has tracked the change speaks to its sophistication.

The Birkman asks executives, "Do others see you as too aggressive or too submissive?" To be successful, bosses have to find the style that best suits the needs not just of the company culture but of various teams, and not just a team as a whole but of each team member. That means moving from the one-style-fits-all leadership model to one that allows you to adopt several styles within your own natural approach.

As with all other Birkman Components, Authority is multidimensional. In addition to revealing how easily a person gives verbal commands, the Authority Component also measures how much a person will tolerate being on the receiving end of strong orders. How much do you actually need, and want, to be bossed? Many people, though they might not readily admit it, prefer a boss who is direct and authoritative. They thrive only when they know who is in charge, feeling most secure with supervisors who let them know what they want done and give some idea of when and how to do it.

These contrasting styles can be seen and measured by Birkman on a Component continuum by looking at the Authority Need. The Birkman will help you determine under which style of Authority you work most effectively, whether you prefer to be led by an in-charge style or by a more self-directed style where you are being asked politely. Many people respond well to direct commands, and just as many prefer some personal autonomy. The low Authority Need types are at their productive best when left in charge of themselves. They prefer to collaborate with a boss who offers suggestions rather than orders, and so work better when the boss is laid back, low key, and less directive.

Most people are a nuanced blend of Authority styles in their preference for leading and being led, and this is clearly seen on the Birkman. A person might have a highly directive personal style (commonly seen in entrepreneurs and solo practitioners) yet not want to be told what to do or how to do it. In just as many cases, a person may be affable and congenial in daily demeanor yet work best with a boss who is clearly in charge and forceful in making decisions and giving orders.

THE DIRECT APPROACH

Jeffrey P. Haggquist, a Washington osteopath specializing in pain and sports medicine, found the Birkman to be reassuring during a time of crisis in his clinic. He is an unapologetic high Authority boss in his small clinic of about nine core employees. His nonmedical staffers, he says, were getting lost when he gave directions, trying to follow them to the letter rather than using what he said as a basis for doing their own problem solving. "People miss the forest for the trees," he says. "They do what I say rather than understanding."

His staff, for their part, felt they were getting mixed messages on what to do—not daring to take the initiative when their boss had been so explicitly and highly directive. They were becoming easily discouraged in their daily routines. The Birkman showed a significant gap between the physician's Authority Usual Behavior and his Authority Need (81 versus 37).

"He would not like to be managed the way he manages," says his consultant, Barbara Robinson. "And he is likely to become domineering and oppositional under stress, given his Authority Stress score of 75."

The doctor wasn't eager to change his approach. The Birkman, however, helped him and his staff members immediately by showing how they might work within the realities of his authoritative leadership style. "Globally, it grounded me in letting me know that I am who I am; it's my personality . . . and that it's okay," he says.

He has decided to hire more staffers who are medically oriented, he says. For any new personnel, he says, he uses his Birkman to explain to them his leadership style and expectations and has them complete the assessment to highlight Issues and Differences to Watch when working with him. He has learned how to prevent confusion and ward off potential issues before they become personal: "I just tell people who I am up front."

Meanwhile, Barbara continues to conduct regular meetings with staff to improve communications and the work environment.

ONE-MAN SHOW

A Houston lawyer with an even higher score on Authority—in the 90s for Usual Behavior—found he had a similar problem in his firm. The fact that he led a two-person staff didn't make communication any easier. In this case, the high score manifested itself in shouting, aggressive behavior, and high-volume commands.

"I want them to know who is in charge," he told Birkman consultant Bob Brewer.

"You're doing that by shouting and being demanding. You're yelling at educated people like they're third-graders," Bob told his client. "They already know who is in charge."

It was hard for the lawyer to change his overbearing behavior. The business was, after all, a one-man show in a firm that bore his name. He seemed to fear that unless he was domineering, he would lose the respect of his staff. "We all have blind spots, and that was his," Bob explains. "It's the way you wound people—verbal clout."

The consultant convinced the lawyer that it was in his best interest to try a more democratic approach. "This was a journey of a thousand steps, or at least several conversations characterized by compassionate candor," Bob says.

Bob coached the attorney to own up to several aspects of his work relationships. First, he had to admit to his tendency to go over the top in the way he gave directions and responded to employees' job performance, which typically failed to meet his standard; second, he had to acknowledge that the staffers' response to his high Authority style was normal, and not the reaction of "wimps who couldn't take the heat," as he described it; and third, he had to acknowledge the Authority Needs of his small staff for a boss who was firm but fair and would offer more suggestions and bark fewer orders. Bob reports that the attorney eventually "made progress in better managing his own 'unrealistic' expectations of others."

The consultant had similar discussions with the staff to help them better manage their responses to their boss's behavior. He coached them to accept their boss for who he is, a work in progress; avoid oversensitivity when he reverted to his high-handed methods; cut him some slack in his efforts to improve; expect progress to come incrementally; and affirm his best efforts to make the changes that everyone wanted to see, "because behavior rewarded is behavior repeated."

"It wasn't a pretty fix," Bob says, "but with patience on the part of the staff and sincere commitment to change on the part of the boss, they discovered how to work together better for mutual benefit."

POWER VERSUS EMPOWERING

It is preferable to take care of Authority issues early on in a professional relationship, before workplace patterns become entrenched. Sonya Shields, executive national vice president for Arbonne, a cosmetics and health and wellness company, needed to hire an assistant who was organized and could take charge of handling day-to-day appointments and paperwork. It seemed a simple task, but she was going through one personal assistant after another. "She would hire people, and they would last three or six months and they'd be gone," says her consultant, Ian Whitfield, of Calgary, Alberta, Canada. "She's a sweet person, so it wasn't that."

Filling a position is never as simple as it seems, because every post is critical, especially for a small company. Sonya runs her business from her home in Canada, doing network marketing and direct sales in four countries. With her husband and two children in the house, the new staff member "had to fit the family," she says.

Her leadership style scores showed a low Usual Behavior score of 37 for Authority with an even lower Need score of 23. "She doesn't use authority as a stick . . . and needs an environment where she is treated warmly and is shown concern for her feelings," says Ian. Sonya's day-to-day style was amiable and cooperative. However, another important aspect of her Birkman results was apparent in her polar-opposite Stress reaction. The Stress score on her Birkman showed she would typically acquiesce if someone became domineering but would "tend to bark" when she felt under pressure and might even explode into self-defense mode if she got pushed too hard, too often.

Also significant was that Sonya's Acceptance score showed she "is great with groups and great with sales . . . but gets her energy back by being by herself or around people she feels close to." She adds, "I tend to be a social person, but [the Birkman] showed me I'd revert at some point and need solitude."

Seeing Sonya's Birkman in detail caused Ian to suggest adding a dimension to the qualities she was seeking in the assistant she wanted to hire. The consultant told Sonya that she didn't need to hire someone with a strong command-and-control style, but she did need someone who would communicate well and not demand much interaction. "A person who was very direct would run over me," Sonya admits. She says the aspect of her Birkman that most surprised her was getting a grasp of her low Authority Need.

The professional recruiter Sonya was using planned to send three candidates, but then asked if he could send a fourth person to give her practice interviewing. Sonya agreed, and had the Birkman consultant sit in on all the final interviews.

The top candidate was experienced and competent, but observing her, Ian guessed her Authority score would be high. She was assertive, very confident, and had the attitude of, "I can,

I can, I can," the consultant says. He watched the candidate interact with Sonya and noticed that the more outspoken the candidate became, the less engaged his client was in the interview.

After the other candidates were interviewed, the fourth, a less experienced young woman, came in. Although she seemed confident enough, she appeared to be a lower Authority type. She was reserved and easy to talk to. Ian saw Sonya lean in during the interview and noted a connection through that body language.

The first candidate would likely "do a great job," Ian suggested to Sonya, but "you'd be walking on eggshells," and it was likely that the candidate would have become just as frustrated by Sonya's lower-key style.

You guessed it: Sonya hired the fourth candidate, who was just there to get practice. She says that knowing her Birkman helped her formulate questions for the candidates about matching values. "Without knowing how I act and who I can work with, I think I would have hired what was on the résumé rather than the person. The Birkman helped me realize I love to empower people. The one I hired was willing to take a pay cut to work for things and people she loved," Sonya says of the inexperienced twenty-three-year-old. "On paper she wasn't as attractive a candidate as she was in person when we interviewed her."

As soon as the woman was hired, Sonya had her fill out a Birkman. "That added depth, because it helped me realize her personality and what drove her. She had to know that I was a boss who would help her strive." She also found out her assistant was a high Structure list person. "So when I want her to do things, I make a list." Armed with her assistant's Birkman, she says, "I know what would be frustrating to her."

"I've done a couple of personality tests," says Sonya, "but this is the one that has hit home in real-life—not just my personality but my needs."

Three years later, the personal assistant was still on the job.

NO ONE SIZE FITS ALL

Some highly capable bosses lead with a low Authority approach. They tend to have a "suggest rather than tell" style, which can also get good results. These are people who prefer to interact with a less direct style of communication. They would much rather make recommendations and suggestions than be required to issue commands or give orders.

Consultant Bob Brewer had to get one boss to master both styles of leadership to direct a small sales team for a home appliances company based in Shreveport, Louisiana.

Joe was "a great sales manager from Oklahoma, a slow-talking, low-key, good ol' boy," is how Bob describes him. He had a low Authority style, preferring a collegial approach to leadership. His reports said they loved it that Joe just made suggestions for how they should work their territories rather than make demands about his own preferences. The sales staff was performing well, except for one salesman who was not part of the boss's fan club and was not as successful as his colleagues.

"I'm not sure he cares," was what the others told the consultant about the salesman.

Then the group's Birkman results came back.

"We look around the room and six of seven all have low Authority Needs," Brewer says. "What we found out was that he was a high Need on Authority."

"I need to know who is in charge," the salesman said, echoing the language on the Birkman report. "Tell me exactly what you want me to do, and I will do it."

It turns out that Joe, because of his leadership style, was leaving this one salesman clueless as to what he had to do to perform well. With a high Authority Need, the salesman understood his boss only when Joe ramped up his Authority image. Bob told Joe that when he spoke to the salesman, he needed to put more authority in his voice and speak in a clear, direct, and commanding way.

"Well, that's not me," the boss protested.

"Joe, you don't have to do it all the time, but see how he needs you to be. Can you do that for him?" Bob asked.

"It won't be comfortable. It won't be natural."

The boss had to work himself up to do it, but when he did, both boss and salesman felt relieved.

THE BIRKMAN AT WORK: EXECUTIVE COACHING

Tremendous amounts of money, effort, and time are spent in corporate training rooms teaching business leaders how to manage, and yet such instruction often fails to become part of the fabric of a corporation, especially in smaller companies. Sometimes the training is missing entirely, the presumption being that hiring the right talent is the end of the effort. But getting the right person in the right job is only the beginning of what can be a complicated and difficult relationship.

Aid to Promotion

John B. Lazar, a Birkman consultant based outside Chicago, finds the assessment is ideal for the executive-coaching engagements he is sometimes asked to do in a limited time frame.

One high-potential midlevel manager in a Chicago utilities company found she needed immediate, if short-term, help when she was being considered for a bigger job in the company. She did well in her current job. She and her three direct reports did mostly technical research and client work. But for her to move higher, she had to improve her communication skills. She wanted to get to the point where she could feel comfortable speaking up during meetings to ask questions and express opinions, and be able to authoritatively set expectations and manage goals for a larger staff. Her moderately low Authority Usual Behavior score (37) suggested she was most comfortable communicating with people using a discuss, suggest, and persuade approach. However, she also needed to expand her range and style to be more direct and directive. Her moderately high Needs score (72) likely meant she needed a boss who would recognize and acknowledge her expertise and strengths. That way, she might be more willing and able to step outside her comfort zone and try new ways of managing. John was called in to help her reach those goals, but he was told he had just five coaching sessions to get his client there. Her Birkman showed she was creative, able to take a long view, and was action oriented. She appeared at ease and motivated when working alone or in small groups, but with her low Need for Acceptance, she tended to avoid meetings. Her low Usual Behavior score in Structure suggested she tended to underestimate the extent to which some on her staff needed the security of greater procedural discipline. She was sensitive in dealing with people (high Usual Behavior scores in Esteem and Empathy) and direct when speaking with people about important issues.

First, John used the Birkman to identify how she might best learn new approaches quickly. The assessment's "how to talk to her" and "the biggest mistakes you can make with her" sections made these suggestions:

- Show appropriate respect.
- Don't be afraid to disagree openly with her.
- Present the big idea first, then wait for a response before offering more detail.
- Don't make the mistake of making her conform unnecessarily.

The assessment also informed him that the client "learns by reading and/or writing."

He then identified how she might act under Stress—for example, "can become silent" in certain situations or, at the opposite extreme, "becomes domineering, even aggressive." He suggested she begin to try new behaviors on the job: speaking up more in group settings and having regular conversations with her direct reports well before a completion deadline to better manage delegated work. Each week she did a self-evaluation of how well she accomplished each of her goals.

John also had her develop her in-the-moment awareness and confront the choices she made. She preferred one-on-one communication and wasn't that fond of groups (high Usual Behavior in Esteem, low Need in Acceptance), so her comfort zone was sitting in her office and working. John pushed her to get out of the office regularly to help her reports.

By their fourth session, the manager had the courage to make a bold choice: she would share her entire Birkman report with her manager. It proved to be a starting point for a deep discussion between the two about how he could best manage her, how he should speak to her. They used the Birkman dialogue reports that address universal topics such as, "the biggest mistakes you can make with her," what motivation she needed to do her best work, and the nature of her learning style.

The client described her conversation with her boss as positive and constructive. The Birkman gave him a deeper understanding of her, and she felt they built a stronger professional connection. With confidence, he gave her opportunities to play a more explicit leadership role, and she shined.

John says he felt proud of his client's quick progress. "I found it stunning that she was able to use the Birkman as a focal point of conversation with her manager—to provide information and to collaborate and seek guidance to be better managed by him," he says.

Perhaps most valuable, John says, was that inside and outside her work environment, she began to recognize the fact that what she needed to operate at her best was different from what other people need to operate. It is a core Birkman concept. The only way to understand that is to get to know others and not assume they are like you, John says.

In their final coaching meeting, John invited the woman's boss to join them for part of the session so they could discuss together what changes had occurred over the two months of coaching. The boss said the manager spoke up in meetings, offered her opinions, and asked questions in ways that engaged others and furthered conversation. She confirmed she was working differently with her direct reports and admitted to the challenges she experienced in beginning new practices. Overall she said her work relationships had changed for the better, although she realized it would take time for the new habits to become routine.

At the end of that final session, her manager said he would be announcing her promotion the following month.

Not Buying the New Boss

A new boss at a large East Coast company was put in charge of about a dozen chemical engineers and research lab technicians. The boss, a man in his early forties who had been put on an executive track, wasn't a scientist, but instead had a solid background in marketing and sales. As often happens, he had a particular knack for managing up and was well liked among his superiors, but he never got much training or the opportunity to learn how to lead a group of employees.

Still, senior management thought he was just what was needed to lead the research team, which had earned a reputation for being sullen, low key, and at times rebellious. The conflict between the manager and his reports was instant and intense. The employees were mistrustful of their new leader and dismissed him as "sales-y" and too much of a lightweight in the scientific arena.

The company asked Pennsylvania consultant Janice Bergstresser to help the new boss improve communication with the team, as well as boost overall cooperation among the team members. She found the boss under siege. "Engineers tend not to praise," Janice says. "They enjoy analysis, tearing things apart to see how they work. The new boss took their comments as personal criticism."

The new leader, a typical high-powered Green, was high Authority in Usual Behavior and liked to talk a lot—he was direct and stuck to the facts. But he was also low Challenge and didn't like hearing criticism. And he had a high Need for Empathy, which he wasn't getting from his staffers, who kept their distance from him. To keep himself fortified against the barrage of negative interaction, he kept a "successes" file to look at when he was feeling low and particularly unappreci-ated. The file had good-news items that he had collected from his years at the company, such as his best performance reviews and letters of appreciation.

The boss's Birkman profile in fact showed that he was direct and blunt when communicating with others, although his personal Needs required others to be sensitive and con-siderate with him. His scores showed he was quick to make decisions, but then had to mull them over long afterward. He appeared easy-going and extroverted, but took the criticism of others as a personal affront and always true. He also scored low on his ability to express his feelings. He had several clear strengths. His biggest asset was that he was a strong Green and could be charming and persuasive. In fact, he consistently did a good job of negotiating on his team's behalf on any number of issues.

Because there was little trust among the group, Janice gave each employee a private Birkman feedback. It gave the individuals a chance to view their own results and understand the Birkman Method process before being asked to share the data—and so build trust. The consultant measured the group's reaction to the information, pointing out group strengths and vulnerabilities and the role those played in achieving certain goals. She also encouraged them to ask questions about the boss.

Meanwhile, she coached the new leader separately. Her first step was to get him to review and challenge his assumptions about the team and how to move forward. Her aim was to get him to internalize a few new steps in his management style. She suggested he

- Provide complete agendas with facts and figures at least one day before meetings so the analyzers could digest, gripe about, and discuss with colleagues.

- Provide more data, not less, in those reports so no points of contention would catch the team by surprise.

- Wait for a consensus and not to expect quick agreement.

- Say to himself, "They are analyzing the idea, not attacking me."

- Delegate heavy analysis and research decisions to direct reports to relieve his daily burden, giving himself final approval.

- Ask more questions by e-mail about upcoming meetings so as not to get worn out listening to endless early analyses and first impressions.

• Study the Birkman group report's "differences to watch" segment between himself and each individual direct report, so he could manage each person as a unique individual and not lump everyone together.

Janice also conducted face-to-face "differences to watch" sessions between the manager and each staffer who asked for it; about half did. Once everyone was comfortable with the individual reports, they agreed to share some of the results. The consultant held two meetings with all in attendance, so they could react to the information, identify their strengths and vulnerabilities, and discuss how their similarities and differences contribute to achieving work goals.

During this process, the team came to the realization that the boss complemented their talents. His ability to communicate easily with upper management was raising the reputation of the unit as a whole and of many of the individuals. They were getting more recognition from above than they ever had in the past. Budgets were approved more often, as were their other requests. The new boss had the negotiating skills they—and their previous boss—had lacked. Understanding their differences as well as their common goals had immediately improved the workplace harmony between the boss and his reports.

7

Are You in It to Win It?

Advantage and Activity

Just how badly do you need to win? What is it you're playing for? Prestige? Money? Status? Making the world a better place?

It's not always easy to answer these questions honestly because of the assumptions associated with each response about the kind of person you are. This is especially true if you grew up in a family or a culture that has strict dictates about the rewards you should seek and frowns on striving only for personal gain.

The Birkman can shed light on your real reward motivation—what is called your Need for Advantage—in a way that is nonjudgmental. Your Birkman result, as always, will fall on a spectrum of reward expectations. In that way, it helps you learn what you really want to be motivated, not what someone tells you should be your reward. It also signals the intensity of your competitive need to win in status, perks, competition, or compensation.

For this discussion on motivation, it is useful to pair your Advantage with your Activity scores. Activity is another way of measuring your physical participation in your work—the degree to which you thrive on moving around. It is important in determining whether you can sit comfortably in a cubicle for a workday—or a whole career!—or whether you need some routine and regular physical activity to feel fulfilled.

These scores, when understood, can help an employer choose the best and most efficient way to offer incentives to employees and keep them engaged. Does the manager reward a sales team for meeting its goals by sending the entire group on a chartered flight to Hawaii? Or do the staff members prefer individual rewards? Employees with lower Advantage Need scores appreciate the first gesture, preferring to work toward a mutually advantageous reward. They don't feel good about beating out their fellow team members to win a prize. They are more inclined to work for the same pay as their colleagues. They aren't as demanding of their employers for special treatment in terms of monetary rewards and perks. They might say, "If they see my good work, they'll want to reward me. I shouldn't have to ask for it." Some would describe them as idealistic because they often have to be pushed to ask for what they deserve.

High Advantage employees want a hierarchy of tangible rewards to stay motivated. They measure self-worth by how they are compensated and have stronger demands than their lower Advantage counterparts. Pay, benefits, and titles are important, but even those prizes aren't enough for some people who seek the biggest piece of the pie. They say, "It's not about us; it's about me. Where is my special reward for special efforts?" Some will see them as too self-seeking or self-protective. People can be effective and successful with either style or anywhere on the Advantage spectrum. From both an individual and a leadership standpoint, what matters is understanding that people respond differently to prestige and monetary incentives.

SOFT SELL IN MEXICO

A consultant at Professional Learning Partners in Mexico City found that varying Advantage scores were behind a concern a boss had about a staff member in the Mexico City office of a large pharmaceutical company based in the United States. The employee was representing the company in tough negotiations for a big sale to a pharmacy chain. Whenever the staffer updated his boss on the negotiations, the manager saw his performance as too much of a soft sell. He "lacked forcefulness and energy," the manager complained to the consultant, Jorge Lara.

Jorge had an idea that the problem was one of perspective, not performance, and checked the Birkmans of the two. Sure enough, the negotiator's Advantage score showed a Need of just 14, compared with his boss's high Need Advantage ranking of 87. The negotiator wasn't timid; he just wasn't interested in "coming out on top in every instance," Jorge says. Rather than scoring a big win, he was aiming for a solution that everyone could live with.

Once his boss understood this thinking, he stopped seeing his report as a failure and instead decided that having such an approach on a team of negotiators that had others playing hardball was a good thing, and he let his report continue his strategy.

Ultimately there is no simple answer to what you might need to keep yourself motivated, and it often isn't easy to admit to what it takes for you to give your all to a task. Consultant Jonathan Michael of Vancouver, Canada, says he "struggled" with his Advantage score when he first took the Birkman. "I grew up in a religious environment, not thinking about myself, being unselfish," he says. In his Usual Behavior, his Advantage score was low, but his Need shocked him: 99. "I am extremely competitive," he now admits cheerfully. After he found out his results, he went to a university to study leadership at nonprofits and admitted to himself to having a goal: to win the highest scholastic award in the school. He won that award—and then others. "I went after it wholeheartedly because of the Birkman," he adds. "I stopped apologizing for wanting a reward. I never negotiated a salary in the past, but now I do."

Over the years, many Birkman consultants have had the opportunity to work with members of all kinds of sports teams. What they discovered, from baseball to basketball to football, is that even for the most highly paid, high-performing, and fiercely competitive athletes, the common denominator among the individual players trended toward a surprisingly low Advantage Need. They had very high Activity scores, as one would expect, but when it came to their Advantage Needs, the players' mind-set was to win for the team rather than for themselves as individuals.

LIKING THAT CUBICLE?

In addition to looking at how motivated you are, or aren't, by the opportunity to win the big prize or seek public accolades, the Birkman also takes a look at what you require to stay physically comfortable—the level of consistent movement you prefer throughout your day. In the Activity Component, we can gauge how necessary it is for you to be in a job that offers some degree of physical effort, as well as how much you demand a kinesthetic outlet for your physical energy.

This is a fancy way of saying that even at a desk job, a high Activity person will tend to get up from the desk and move around as often as possible, perhaps making three trips down the hall to do three errands, whereas lower Activity folks are good at conserving their energies and might stay more anchored to the office chair, perhaps rising only after combining several tasks into one trip down the hall.

Identifying your physical Activity Need is another way the Birkman will help you and your employer figure out how to make the best use of your energies. Do you conserve your energy, or do you need outlets throughout the day to get rid of the antsy feeling that long days at the computer can generate? You might get more done on the walk to lunch than at the lunch itself. Many business leaders have talked about getting their best ideas during their morning exercise routines.

The Activity Component, however, isn't addressing your workouts at the gym; in fact, many people who have low Activity scores are diligent about their exercise routines. Rather, this Component gives insight as to what degree you are likely to regularly need an outlet to express your physical energies throughout the day in order to be at ease and to thrive.

As with each of the other Birkman Components, there are pluses that accompany each score wherever it appears on the spectrum. But each Birkman Need score also carries with it a potential trap that is its flip side. Both behavioral styles are essential, but both can do damage when out of control.

AN UNEXPECTED FACTOR

Consultant Peter Capodice of Sarasota, Florida, found the Activity score to be a significant—and unexpected—factor when he was helping an emerging dry cleaning franchisor based in the Chicago area find a director of marketing. "We're small, so the head of marketing would be *the* person," says Michael Corrao, the chief operating officer for the company, CD One Price Cleaners.

Over several months, the company had hired two new marketing individuals, and both had failed in the position. The first person lasted twelve months, the second even less than that. The hiring errors were costly in both the actual cost of salary and benefits—hundreds of thousands of dollars—and the intangible cost of time and stress. The senior managers couldn't figure out why the people who were hired weren't working out, so Peter conducted Birkmans with the CEO and his four top executives to help them communicate with each other internally before they tried to bring in another director.

All four executives had certain distinctive traits, including high Activity numbers. The lowest Activity score on the team was 66, and the average was 76. The consultant saw this as one reason that the team, which had a special dynamic of using a thoughtful, qualitative approach to decision making, also possessed the ability to move quickly once a decision was made. Their high-energy approach was needed at the time because the business wanted to make an aggressive marketing push in an industry that is especially competitive.

Peter says he typically discourages management from hiring too many people like themselves, but he also subscribes to the model that says too many differences, especially with an immediate superior, can thwart the chances for success for someone newly hired. "Yes, you want a change, or someone different from you, but we don't want you calling me back in ninety days," he told them. "Too much divergence will diminish productivity and organizational effectiveness."

Peter had the C-suite executives help him map out which duties were tied to certain Birkman Components and Interests and so they were able to match the Birkman results with existing corporate culture, one element of which was the high Activity score. His strategy was to find candidates with skills that would complement the talent that already existed in the company while fitting into the overall office culture.

The executives did a series of interviews to whittle down the candidate list and then had the three finalists take the Birkman to help with the overall review among the group. Then the hiring team did extensive final interviews. "As we interviewed candidates, it was interesting to see where the differences were between them and the team," says Michael.

"The individual they hired was a high Activity Need, although not quite as high as the overall group, and early indications are that it is a good fit," Peter says. After the candidate was hired, the consultant helped coach the staff on how they might work together to ensure success.

MEANINGFUL WORK

The president of an Atlanta-based property management firm wanted his director of sales and marketing to take the Birkman because she wasn't getting up to speed in her job. Management saw only that she didn't have a good image of a salesperson. She regarded any sales professional as "like being a used-car salesman," consultant Steve Cornwell recalled. No one in the organization was able to mentor her.

When Steve looked at her Advantage score, he found she had a high Advantage Need, suggesting she wanted recognition for a job well done. She also had very high Social Service (99) and Persuasive (92) Interests. "So for her to truly enjoy her work, she needed to know that what she was selling was also helping others," he says.

Not getting proper recognition for her work and not understanding the good it was doing for the public lowered her opinion of her job. By understanding her Birkman scores, her boss learned how to meet her needs and better motivate her. He gave her feedback for jobs well done and explained to her that selling wasn't just to push a product but to benefit people in need of a service. Reframing her role in this way worked for her. The director was able to embrace that notion and adopted a happier and more confident attitude toward her sales team. The company president told the consultant that the Birkman coaching and subsequent sales sessions helped the company's performance significantly in just a few months.

SENSITIVE TO SELLING

Dave Agena's first exposure to Birkman was as a senior executive at one of the largest mortgage banking operations in the United States. He wanted to get a picture of the top 10 percent of his account executives so he could use that as a template to recruit new personnel. He took the Birkman and reviewed the results with a consultant.

"I was mortified!" says Dave. "I didn't fit the stereotype of what I felt a high-performance and highly competitive national sales executive ought to look like!"

His high Esteem scores made him look too sensitive in light of the image he had of himself as a tough national sales manager. His overall Usual Behavior on the Life Style Grid was Blue and not the more typical Red/Green that is associated more with a commission-driven sales job. He also had what the Birkman calls a reversal in his Advantage score, which is rare. That means he would tend to ask for individual rewards when he really wanted to be evaluated based on team performance—except when he did exceptionally well and wanted the recognition. In that case, he worried he was sabotaging his authentic participation in either a commission-based or a team-based reward system. "I don't mind doing things for the team if everyone is pulling their weight, because I have adopted an altruistic worldview," he says. "Unfortunately, that doesn't always mix well in a commission-sales culture."

He soon realized that what he considered his weaknesses were in fact his strengths. Consultant Claire Carrison showed him that he was an effective executive precisely because he related to a wide variety of people and knew how to give them the proper incentives. His effective style was to get people to buy into an idea rather than to push them. The advice served him well enough that he had a successful career in mortgage banking and then cofounded two management consulting firms.

"I have a high degree of emotional intelligence, which I didn't understand until I took the Birkman," says Dave, who eventually became a Birkman consultant himself. "It was like hearing yourself on a tape recorder for the first time or seeing yourself in a video for the first time. You don't recognize yourself at first."

A FRATERNITY'S ADVANTAGE

A college campus was having a problem with one of its fraternities, whose members were always getting into trouble with out-of-control parties and breaking a slew of university rules—about as many as they could. The fraternity had been on probation for some time and were about to get kicked off campus when Wilson Wong of Atlanta was asked to help. The consultant gave Birkmans to forty-six of the fraternity brothers.

The most striking aspect of their results was how high their Advantage scores were across the board, meaning they were driven by the promise of personal gain. They were so competitive that they were enjoying being the best at being bad! "We are all competitive, whether it's just with our own past or with others," Wilson says.

The consultant knew he had to give them a new focus for their rewards, which at their age still had to result in being noticed and gaining recognition. "On a college campus, Advantage is all about reputation—to be perceived as the best of the best, not only by peers but by the university."

Wilson persuaded the fraternity members that each one of them would gain even greater notice and reputation if they focused their considerable competitive energies—they tended toward high Activity Need scores as well—on doing good. Then they would be both respected and be perceived as trailblazers. "They loved that," he says.

The fraternity became more involved in campus activities and community work. They still threw plenty of parties, but they were responsible parties. After a while, their good deeds started to get them noticed, and even their parties were considered some of the best on campus. They started to win the praise of their campus peers and the university administration. Now, a couple of academic years later, they still are considered role models for how to run a fraternity. Wilson had helped the campus shape what a reward should look like for the students while acknowledging their high Advantage Needs.

THE BIRKMAN AT WORK: DIVERSITY

The Birkman philosophy is that individuals are complex, each one possessing important strengths that are of great value to any workplace once they are unlocked. In the bigger picture, it teaches an appreciation of the value of others and the knowledge that the strength of the whole lies in the variety of strengths of the participants. That philosophy is at the heart of the push for diversity, which most big companies define in broad terms to include gender, race, ethnicity, religion, experience, age, and a number of personal challenges. The effort to achieve greater diversity is thwarted when we stop seeing the individual and instead make a broad, quick judgment based on a first glance. The Birkman forces us to take a deeper look to see what drives and motivates individuals and how we fit together in the workplace.

Seeing the Individual

The head of diversity and leadership development for a Fortune 500 food company says the Birkman has been a valuable tool for helping to advance her company's diversity and inclusion efforts.

"We talk about diversity layers," she says. "The first things you see in a person might be black, white, man, woman, older, younger. But that's not how business gets done or how work is valued." The Birkman Method, she adds, gets people to connect with colleagues on the commonalities as well as their differences—"he likes to work alone"; "I like to work in groups"—and to see color only in terms of Red, Blue, Yellow, and Green and the valuable contributions to the work process those Birkman colors represent. "With the Birkman, all types are valued, so it generates a fast and deep level of trust so we can move to the next level," she says.

Their employees start to speak in Birkman's inclusive language. "At our company, we use the 'range not change' approach," she explains. "You don't change who you are, but develop a broad range of perspectives and skills to work collaboratively with those people who might be very different from you. We strive to really value that range. It unlocks the diversity of our working teams and accelerates innovation and problem solving."

Patti Corbett Hansen, one of the Birkman consultants who has worked extensively with her company, has helped develop reports and team session formats that have enabled the diversity and leadership development team to maximize the value of their assessments. "These types of leadership development resources are impacting our culture in a positive way," the diversity chief says, "and creating a culture where the best of all groups can succeed."

On a case-by-case basis, the Birkman reminds us that no one can solve a complicated question with an easy answer. The director of diversity and leadership development in the human resource department of the same company recalls a problem that arose when team members began clashing with one of their directors. They began to see the problem as a diversity issue, believing that it stemmed from the fact that the team director was foreign born and so must have a different way of exerting his authority. But once the group took a look at their Birkmans, they could see why the director seemed abrasive—and it was no different from a number of their own results. He had low Esteem and low Empathy in Usual Behavior but high Needs, pointing to his dominant managing style but little tolerance in being treated by people the way he treated them.

"It got to the why and the how," the director says. "The Birkman shows how complex every individual is, and that if we try to stereotype, we miss it, because a lot of what makes a person tick is making sure his or her needs are met. We truly have to know an individual to connect with and understand the person."

It's the Similarities

That story would ring true to Beroz Ferrell, a Kent, Washington, consultant who used the Birkman to resolve what had seemed to be a culture clash in a nonprofit organization. The conflict was between two employees and was becoming disruptive to the organization as a whole. "When I sat down with each of them, it was perceived that they were so different from each other—one a United States–born woman and one an Asia-born woman," says Beroz.

"Interestingly they were clearly different in styles," she says, "but it was their similarities that were creating the conflict. Their Esteem Need scores were the same—both high—as was their Empathy Need scores. They were both very sensitive and were just trying to get needs met in different ways."

A conflict that was initially blamed on ethnic differences was just a typical difference between two people with differing needs and work styles. The American woman had a Usual Behavior style that made her seem confident and self-assured, but under stress, she tended to allocate blame to others. The Asian woman had a profile that suggested she tended to second-guess herself a lot and took on responsibilities for people and events more than she needed to. "These differences perpetuated the two not seeing eye-to-eye and always getting irritated by one another's style differences," Beroz says.

The Birkman dug below the stereotypes to reveal the individuals and counter the myth of clashing cultures. "We tend to think our most visible differences are the things that are creating the challenges," Beroz says. "We say, 'Well it's our race, our background, or because we are men and women who don't understand each other.' But research implies it's really style differences that get in the way unless we are conscious about them. So let's see our different styles in Birkman, and from that understand the other dimensions of diversity."

8

How Your Emotions Can Help or Hurt a Decision

Empathy and Thought

The stereotype of corporate America is that it is a sterile environment that turns its denizens into robots going about their daily routines with extraordinary efficiency. Anyone who works in an office knows, of course, that it is an emotional, political, and volatile landscape where productivity and efficiency can be derailed by any number of problems.

Understanding how much emotion and how much thought people put into their decision making can help us navigate many of the land mines in that perilous landscape. Empathy and Thought are two critical Components that show us some of the give-and-take that go into how choices are made.

Empathy is about how you are seen expressing your feelings, and it helps you understand how others will express theirs. It can measure how we process emotion, the degree to which we enjoy being emotionally expressive, and how we ultimately are energized by our emotions. The Need score for the Empathy Component is an important window on our behavior and offers a useful way to help us see some critical differences in how we relate to each other. We pair it with the Need for the Thought Component, which measures the speed of our decision making and the amount of detail we want before we are comfortable in coming to a decision.

You may be thinking that you have finally stumbled across what could potentially be a "bad" score! After all, no one wants to be seen in the workplace as a drama queen. But by now you have learned to appreciate the advantages of being at any point on the 1–99 Birkman scoring span. And so it is with Empathy: there is no better or worse way to be. Six decades and several million people in the Birkman database confirm that people fall all along the Empathy continuum and that having a wide variety of emotional responses provides enormous social benefit to us as a society. You can easily understand how having empathy can be seen as a virtue in any setting.

Obviously we all care, and we all have feelings. The Empathy Component is not about whether we have feelings; it is about recognizing our comfort levels with expressing our emotions and how much we enjoy emotional demonstrativeness. The significance here is to be aware of whether a person chooses to heighten and express his or her emotions or would rather minimize and play down those emotions. Our contrasting styles and needs in this area matter greatly in our self-management, relationships with others, and selection of careers.

The Need for Empathy spectrum can describe the more nuanced aspects of our feelings so we can recognize, acknowledge, and understand these contrasts. As with every other

Birkman Component, the majority of us fall somewhere toward the center of extremes, but it is easier to talk about black and white than shades of gray. We will look at some extreme examples of Empathy scores to help describe the significance of the Component and point out where the most intense scores might open the potential for tripping up, especially in dealing with people with sharply contrasting tendencies.

ONCE WITH FEELING

High Empathy people are deeply connected to and keenly aware of their emotionality. Employees who rank high on the Component are seen as expressive, enthusiastic, passionate, and more likely to use emphasis and colorful language than is typical. In other words, they can be fun to be around! Any industry can reap the rewards of having such a person on staff who is able to make an emotional connection with clients or enthusiastically warm up a room. In particular, high Empathy qualities can pay huge dividends in activities that are intuitive and performance-based, including writing, singing, speaking publicly, and arguing a legal case.

A high Empathy style also can be volatile, especially when it combines with a high Authority style in Stress mode. Then we are likely to hear a message delivered with a great deal of emotional force and in a loud voice. What is important is to find productive ways to acknowledge the real emotional Needs of the higher Empathy types who want to be heard without compromising the work and goals of others.

The Birkman has the ability to show a deeper view of behavior on multiple levels: Usual Behavior, Needs, and Stress. The potential downside of this gift of emotionality is that in a Stress mode, high Empathy people can feel discouraged or even become depressed. They can more easily find themselves stalled in Stress mode, swamped by their own feelings and finding it difficult to take action. Ironically, taking action or doing positive activity such as physical exercise or helping someone else can be an antidote. It is one of the most effective ways to overcome this kind of emotional inertia.

PLAYING IT COOL

The Birkman also can crack the facade to find where a low Empathy person might be hiding a need for more emotion, that is, a desire for a warm and sympathetic response. You may exhibit a low Usual Behavior Empathy style in your workplace environment, for example, but when you go home, you find you're able to process your higher Empathy Needs by relying on the sympathetic ear of a spouse or a friend. In figure 8.1, the person would tend to show little emotion with others and would prefer that people also treat him or her in a direct and practical way, leaving emotions aside. Problems could arise if this person were under Stress and became too dismissive of what others are feeling, demanding they just "get over it."

Low Empathy people come across as matter-of-fact, logical, and in control of their emotions, sometimes to the point of a certain cool detachment, preferring to avoid what they view as excessive drama. Birkman consultants and other researchers have noted the generational shift over the decades toward more detached outward behavior among those with an MBA, at least in their Usual Behavior but not necessarily in their Needs. Also, although women are often thought to be more

Figure 8.1 The Empathy Component

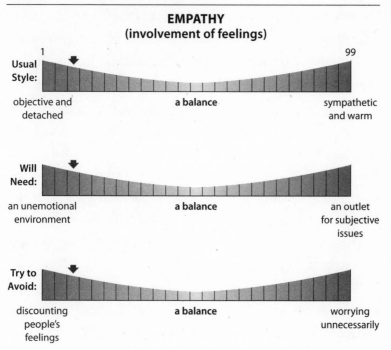

emotional, Birkman research shows there is no gender connection with respect to this Component trait.

The gift of the low Empathy approach is the ability to choose to get on with it by offering practical solutions and immediate action to remedy a situation. The lower your score is, the less you need verbal sympathy. In fact, that approach may annoy you and even make you suspicious. For you, it is "just the facts, ma'am," with little need for sympathy or histrionics. You can see how this quality is essential for those doing work that requires objective responses and quick, level-headed action, especially for, say, airline pilots and neurosurgeons. Most paramedics and emergency medical technicians are low Empathy because they have to detach, even though they are certainly caring, helpful people.

Low Empathy people may clash with someone who isn't seeking such immediate action but is craving a sensitive ear to hear them out without offering a solution. They may frustrate their higher Empathy colleagues by saying, "Just fix it," or, "Come back when you're better."

HIDDEN FEELINGS

Low Empathy people also care deeply about others and have strong emotions. What Birkman is measuring with this Component is how they choose to deal with those emotions, and the extent to which they let them play a role in their interactions.

One consultant was surprised by how Empathy turned around discussions when she gave the Birkman to six top executives at a Kansas construction company. She was working with the members of the leadership team to ensure their goals and plans of action for the company were aligned so they could work together effectively. Suddenly, during a feedback session, one of the men seemed thrown off by his very low Empathy score—10 in his Usual Behavior and the same for Need. His concerns were separate from anything going on at work, but could be critical to how he kept up his energy and motivation for the job. He had just finished what he referred to as "an ugly and bitter divorce" in which he had partial custody of his sons and was worried this score meant he would have a hard time connecting with them, the consultant says. "He was on the verge of tears," says Stacey Mason, an Arkansas-based consultant. "If I would have had the stereotypical idea about construction workers, I would have been wrong."

She explained to the group that the low score was more about how the executive was showing his feelings than it was about what he actually felt. "To have a low score, whether in Usual Behavior or Need, means we show Empathy in a very practical way," she says. His low scores also meant that he saw himself as "just as emotional as the average person—no more or less," and, moreover, he wouldn't stay down if he got a little down.

The man's colleagues all chimed in and told him that they saw him as kind and considerate. "He got a lot of love," says Stacey. "They were a close group, but the Birkman gave them the opportunity to have something measurable to guide the conversation."

They used the Birkman as a jumping-off place rather than as a tool for baring their souls. They reached a level where they got to say what they wanted to say without either posturing or using emotional language.

TOO TOUCHY-FEELY?

It isn't always the case that your colleagues will be open to discussing your home life in the office or seek to strengthen personal ties. A newly assembled team for a luxury-homes service in Atlanta discovered after taking the Birkman that five of the seven group members had similar Empathy scores: low in both Usual Behavior and Need. One member had low Usual Behavior and moderate Need. The newest member of the team stood out from the pack, scoring high on both.

The overall culture in the workplace was informal, but also rather impersonal in conducting daily work, says consultant Steve Cornwell. They cut to the chase on issues, big and small, typically acting in an objective and practical way.

The one high Empathy team member, in contrast, was very personable, and being new, she went out of her way to be nice to the others. "She would send thank-you cards for little things and never missed bringing a birthday card or making a big deal about special events," says Steve. "She was the first to say, 'Good morning' and 'Good night.'"

Her extreme cheerfulness rubbed the others the wrong way. They were suspicious of the new employee's motives and felt her actions were at worst fake and at best showed that she was trying too hard. She could hardly say a word without the rest of the group rolling their eyes, the consultant says. "We don't like that warm and fuzzy stuff here!" one team member said in a separate meeting with the consultant. "We are all here to do a job, and that's it. We're not looking to be everyone's best friend."

Steve called a team meeting to review the Birkman scores of each member. He had plotted a group graph that showed each individual's Needs scores for every Component as a dot labeled with his or her initials. He went through each of the eleven Component scores one by one.

"When we landed on the Empathy Component, it was amazing to see the team's reaction," Steve says. They were shocked by how much of a difference there was between the average score and the new employee's ranking. They also quickly realized how much they had ganged up on her.

"When I explained how this played out, the high Empathy team member exclaimed, 'Finally!' with tears in her eyes—no surprise," Steve says with a laugh. "For the first time, the group could see what she had been up against."

The team members agreed that they had been too harsh with her on many occasions. They never gave a thought about how their treatment must have felt to her and what the collective impact that had had on her. And because the Birkman always seeks balance, the high Empathy team member also was instructed on how she escalated the problem by not staying objective and practical when interacting with team members who clearly didn't appreciate her special efforts.

"We were able to talk through how to best work together moving forward," the consultant says. "By the end of the team session, the group was joking about the differences, and even a few hugs were shared—instigated by you know who!"

THINK ABOUT IT

Low Thought people are speedy decision makers and tend to be proud of that skill. In many aspects of business and government work, the ability to make a decision quickly is highly prized. It is vital for functioning in a just-in-time economy and in times of crisis. But being too impulsive is a danger, especially to someone in a leadership position. It's the ready-fire-aim mentality.

Meanwhile, due diligence is a good thing, but overthinking can shift from prudent caution to outright anxiety, especially in the workplace where a staff member is waiting for directions to proceed with the task at hand. If you rank in the middle of the spectrum, it means your decision making may be fast at times and slower at times—in other words, dependent on the situation or circumstances. Midrange scores in general tend to be less of an issue for most people. Sometimes you might overthink, and sometimes you're quick.

One San Francisco employee found his job on the line when his boss viewed his rapid decision-making style as reckless. The man was a treasurer in a large mortgage firm. His boss, an executive vice president, was sure the controller wasn't doing sufficient due diligence on important decisions and began to consider replacing him with someone who would be more careful.

The boss called in consultant Claire Carrison, who had experience coaching many executives away from the extreme edges of the Thought spectrum. She advised him not to make any final decision until both he and the treasurer took the Birkman. "Let's see if we can get a better picture here of what's going on," she told the anxious executive.

As she suspected, the Birkman showed the vice president had very high Thought scores—in the 90s—for both Usual Behavior and Need and took his time in reaching every decision. That made him suspicious of any one of his reports who didn't go through the same long and detailed process. His treasurer had lower-than-average Thought scores. In Claire's deeper discussions with them, she learned the treasurer hadn't actually made any wrong decisions, but simply had created that suspicion because of his style of working. "Once the EVP saw the numbers proved their decision-making styles were at polar opposite ends, he understood it was not about wrong—it was about *different*," says Claire. The treasurer's job was spared.

ANALYSIS PARALYSIS

Many bosses are plagued with extreme behavior at the other end of the spectrum—being stymied by anxious overthinking of every decision. Nancy Thompson, a Birkman-certified coach at Procter & Gamble in Cincinnati, learned how disruptive the analysis-paralysis executive can be when her company was consolidating job responsibilities for its logistics group.

She conducted Birkmans with the whole logistics leadership team. One member was known to be a foot dragger at meetings and the Birkman showed why: he had a high Usual Behavior score of 92 for Thought, whereas the rest of the team ranged between 6 and 18. The high scorer liked to talk—and talk and talk—through all the details before making a decision.

"I had observed many times how Alex [not his real name] would derail a meeting with long, circular discussions of what everyone else had already said," says Nancy. "His reputation was known to most people, and they would disengage immediately when he started talking" despite the fact that he was knowledgeable and had concrete and valuable contributions to make to the discussions.

Nancy decided to use a visual exercise as an icebreaker. She had the team use exercise stretch bands to illustrate just how different Alex's thought process was from everyone else's. She wasn't that optimistic about how the session would play out, she says, given the entrenched habits of the team and the hostility that had already built up. But the visual device worked. Alex's colleagues saw the sharp contrast and became suddenly sympathetic to the nature of their colleague, and Alex saw just how taxing his process was to the office environment.

Alex was quiet for much of the day during the Birkman sessions, resisting his usual urge to restate everything everyone else said. Finally, he held up his hand and asked, "I know I am usually the 'hitch in the get-a-long' and I promise not to do that, but could I just step in here and say a few words?"

Everyone stopped writing and put pens down and turned to face him. The room listened courteously and attentively while Alex spoke.

"Those with the low Usual scores had recognized how to be respectful of Alex's style," says Nancy. "I am going to guess that this was the first time in years that Alex was able to command that kind of attention."

After several minutes, Alex said, "Okay. That is what I wanted to say."

From that point on, the consultant says, he never again resorted to his former, painfully detailed speechmaking.

ROOM TO PONDER

The Thought Component was also significant for Bayley Kessler, a Lacey, Washington, entrepreneur who had been trying to launch her own florist and jewelry-making business for some years. Her Birkman revealed clues as to why she was having such a hard time advancing: her Thought score topped the charts with a high 99 in Usual Behavior, and her Need score was also high: 84. "Such a high score is super-thoughtful—not demanding a decision," says Jenny Capella, a consultant who also happens to be Bayley's sister and welcomed the opportunity to use the process to strengthen family bonds.

Whenever Bayley had to ponder a question or respond to a request, she often would fall silent. Jenny would mistake the silence for confusion and begin to offer more and more information, which drove her sister into deeper stress and even more analysis paralysis.

After getting her Birkman feedback, Bayley realized she needed plenty of room to think and began to ask for the time she needed to make a decision. "Now we have an agreement," she says. "When Jenny asks me a question, I say I am "99-ing it (because of my high Thought score). She now knows that I am thinking and doesn't feel compelled like before to give more information because I am not answering her right away."

Both sisters were surprised that Bayley also had a very high Usual Behavior score for Empathy and a much lower score for Need. The Usual Behavior made sense because of her empathetic nature. But when Jenny tried to support her by being strongly sympathetic if anything went wrong, Bayley would get frustrated.

"What she needed was logic—grounded, practical logic," says Jenny. "All those years of misinterpreting her actions!"

With those pieces of information, Bayley has become more confident about her business acumen. "Knowing so much more about my process, I can talk about my business with greater confidence," she says.

Also giving her confidence were her art and mechanical scores—both very high—showing that her combination floral and jewelry designer business made perfect sense.

The transformation, says Jenny, was startling. "It was dramatic, and it remains dramatic to this day . . . She is flourishing, doing things with her own steam and on her own time." That transformation also helped the sisters nurture their own relationship.

FAMILY TIME

The Thought process as measured by the Birkman Component can play a role in everyday activities and relationships. Ron Baker of Ontario was able to show a couple—Dr. Ervis Duardo Perez and his wife, Tamara Pina—in a social setting how the Thought Component works.

"How he makes a decision was a main point," says Tamara. "In a crisis, I have an idea, or a decision, for the moment. Ervis takes a long time to make a decision, but once he does, nothing can move him. I'm quicker, but I can change my mind."

In Birkman language, that meant he scored high for Thought in both Usual Behavior and in Need. "It's behind-the-scenes deep thinking," Ron says of Ervis. His wife was low Thought.

Ron laughs about going out to dinner with the couple after one session. "In sixty seconds [Tamara and I] had our order ready," recalls Ron. "Ervis sent away the waitress when she came. Then he sent her away again. Then he sent her away again. I said, 'Do you see how this works?'"

THE BIRKMAN AT WORK: THE GLOBAL WORKPLACE

The Birkman Method is helping to change the discussion on integrating the global workplace, aiming to focus less on cultural differences and more on individual similarities. People are more alike than they are different. Put another way, the differences among individuals in any particular nationality are much greater than any differences among nationalities.

Yet issues of diversity get complicated on a global level because of the sheer breadth of diversity and because we have to recognize and be respectful of different customs and learned behavior. Failing to factor in these differences can trip up people trying to do business or get a job in places that are unfamiliar.

Birkman's database of more than 3 million test takers in twenty-two languages from fifty countries confirms that test results aren't that different from country to country. The differences that we expect to see and that show up in results tend to be in the visible, Usual Behavior, more than in Needs, Interests, or Stress. The differences we have to acknowledge are how those results are interpreted. We have discussed the "easier to dish out than to take it" score (low Usual Behavior, high Need in the Esteem measure of one-on-one communication). That score is more common in North American profiles, where being candid is taught and direct language is prized. In other cultures, where people might be expected to speak more carefully and respectfully to others, Usual Behavior typically shows up as less direct, though Needs will be the same. There are many such cultural differences.

A Focus on Culture

Tasneem Virani, a consultant in London, likes to coach "people as people," she says. She believes the variety of experiences and cultures that so many people are exposed to in today's increasingly connected world makes it harder than ever before to label people. To understand how complex personality and culture can get, she uses the example of her own family: she is an ethnic Indian born in Kenya who studied in England, where her children were born. But the family then lived in the United States, where the children continue to reside. "I can't say they are like me," she says of her children, "because they have more the culture of the United Kingdom, Europe, and the United States, so they are the third culture. If you look at all that, you just have to look at them as human beings."

It gets just as complex in her work. About 75 percent of the coaching she does involves people who have settled in the United Kingdom after living elsewhere in the world—sometimes making more than one stop along the way. "Their values are different, but their personalities speak the same language," she says.

That is, she can verify that few differences among cultures show up on the Birkman, with the exception of some similarities within nationalities in people's Usual Behavior—their learned expressions of certain values and traditions. She finds, for example, that people of Indian, Pakistani, and Middle Eastern backgrounds, among others, tend to have Advantage scores that are low Usual Behavior. They are relieved when their personal demands appear to be modest, Tasneem says. In the same vein, they can be self-conscious when they get a high Need for Advantage score and have to own up to wanting material rewards for their work. To break the news to them about their high score, Tasneem says, she explains to them: "You want to be acknowledged for your work and to know that there are other opportunities for growth."

Tasneem found, however, that even strong cultural values can take a backseat in a workplace environment that is seen as falling short of expectations. She was hired in 2012 to help 4C Hotels Group, a family business based in London, through its corporate relaunch and planned expansion. The family is ethnic Indian; the founding partner was born in Tanzania, and his son was born in the United Kingdom.

Most of the staff of 150 UK employees were recent immigrants from around the European Union and Southeast Asia. Their entry-level jobs in the company, as in the industry as a whole, tended to be low paying, and the employees were getting frustrated over a lack of opportunity. "You could see the problem in recruitment and retention," says Al-karim Nathoo, associate director at 4C Hotel. Turnover was high.

As might be expected, of the twenty who took the Birkman—most from India, Pakistan, and Romania—eighteen showed low Usual Behavior scores in their Advantage Component, which Tasneem says made it easy for them to work for the benefit of all rather than for themselves. But far from being apologetic about their high Needs scores, the employees embraced their wish for rewards for their work. And they let it be known in subsequent discussions that they needed a clearer path to job advancement. Tasneem also saw through the Birkman that many staffers ranked high on the Empathy Component in Need for emotion and expressiveness; in fact, they told her they felt they weren't getting enough feedback from management about their work and didn't have outlets to express their opinions.

While some of the employees wondered if their experience was because of their status as new arrivals in the country, the real issue turned out to be related to corporate culture and had nothing to do with nationality. "There was not a defined culture in the company," says Al-karim. He didn't want such issues to weigh on the future growth of the business. His family was hoping to expand their ten-year-old company into East Africa, he says, and to build new properties. His father, a founding partner in the company, already had expanded the business from a small bed-and-breakfast concern to one that owns ten budget and midmarket hotels—brands such as Holiday Inn Express and Comfort Inn—with shares in similar concerns. "But our processes are still toward mom-and-pop business, and we want to strengthen operations, and focus on human resources and leadership development," says Al-karim.

Tasneem says Al-karim's high Interests in Social Service told her he was sincere about wanting to help his employees and improve their career development, as well as to boost his customer-service performance. The other top managers' Birkman profiles showing a desire to work for the good of the whole, she adds, meant they also could take the steps needed to change the core business culture.

They acknowledged they had to address the company's narrow bench at the upper ranks in terms of variety of work strengths. "We are very numbers oriented, but we don't have a lot of strategic thinkers except for my father and me," says Al-karim. "To grow, we need to bring in other types of people, especially in the sales and marketing side and the softer skills in communication and sales."

To the director, it was clear what the next stage should be: development for those identified on the Birkman as needing training. With Tasneem's help, they began to outline training goals aimed at improving leadership and management skills. "We defined the values and mission of the company, which includes them being more customer focused," Tasneem says. "The key is really to help us all to become more emotionally intelligent by increasing our self-awareness of cultures, of values, but also of personality. Then *you* understand what *I'm* feeling and get to know me, my values, and my culture."

Same Score, Different Meaning

Stephan Altena, a Munich-based Birkman consultant and executive trainer, tells of when he gave Birkmans to an Italian team. As they went over the feedback reports, he pointed out someone in the group who preferred working alone. In the United States, such a preference would barely be noticed, he says. Colleagues would think, "That person likes to work alone. Okay." But in Italy, the employee's teammates were puzzled. It raised suspicion, and the employee's closest colleagues were a little hurt, if not insulted. They asked Stephan to explain: "Why does he want to work alone? Doesn't he like us? Is something wrong?" It was a score that could offend in a culture that emphasizes community and close personal relationships. Scores can be identical, but how they are seen and accepted may change with the cultural context.

Jan Brandenbarg, a senior consultant in the Netherlands, describes an instance in which he was sitting next to a Japanese man who had the same Birkman score as he did for candor and directness: low Usual Behavior for Esteem. He told the other man he was surprised because he seemed to be very careful in how he communicated. "He replied to me, 'You should hear how my colleagues speak of me as being so direct; even my mother says so.'" The source of the differences is complex,

Jan adds. "It has a lot to do with tradition, history, and also with things such as mental programming—which happens when we are young—and history and values. The range of scores is very similar, but the interpretation is not." He sees Authority as one of the Components that has to be closely examined when dealing with multicultural issues, as he often does in his company. He has clients across Europe that can have a single C-suite line-up with nationals from the Netherlands, France, Germany, Belgium, and Poland. Different cultures generally have different levels of respect for Authority and different ways of showing that respect, he says.

Jan, who bases his opinion on the work of Geert Hofstede, the Dutch researcher on culture, considers the acceptance of authority a measure of the distance of a person to the center of power. For example, the distance between the power center and its people is much greater in China than in Northern Europe. The Dutch, Jan says, feel strongly about their standing in corporate and other hierarchies. They say, "You may be the manager, but as a person, we are equal." So you get a strong sense of an egalitarian playing field. In China, a person may be less likely to see an authority figure as an equal. "I interpret the Birkman scores in that light," Jan says.

Your New Boss

Some people are surprised to find that a corporation—an entity they think of as a place lacking in culture and custom—can be faithful to the culture and traditions of its own or its host country.

Tony Swift, general manager for human resources at Hyundai Motor Co. in Sydney, Australia, helped one employee who was having a hard time getting his career started in the marketing department of the Korean-owned company. The new hire, an Australian, was seen as uncooperative, "a cowboy," Tony says. He wasn't fitting in to the company culture, which is very hierarchical.

"Here, when things are asked for by a deadline, they are done. End of story," says Tony. When he gave the employee the Birkman, it showed he had a very high 98 score for Freedom, signaling a strong need for individual expression, and his Structure Need was low, meaning he didn't like to have a lot of rigid processes to follow.

"It was a light-bulb moment," says Tony. "He said, 'Now I get it and understand the problem.'" But it did raise the question: "What was he doing in a Korean organization that is very structured, process oriented, and hierarchical?" He was given a course of action and the opportunity to try to adjust to the corporate culture, but ultimately he decided to find a company culture better suited to his personality.

Seeing the Individual

Heifer International staffers were concerned about issues within one of its leadership teams in southern Africa. The global nonprofit, based in Little Rock, Arkansas, helps communities fight poverty and hunger by giving gifts of living animals along with training that families use to improve their lives.

On the team were four individuals from two different regions, says a manager, who asked that the country not be named. Heifer International had successfully used the Birkman to address differences between staff members in the United States, and it hoped it could be a valuable tool elsewhere.

When the four members of the team took the Birkman, results showed the team leader's style was to be very frank and direct. In fact, he registered about as low on the Esteem scale as possible—a 3 Usual Behavior and a 3 Need! The rest of the team had much higher Needs (79, 79, and 44) for personal and supportive individual contact. "The team leader also tested a low Needs Acceptance style, or low sociability, so he saw no reason to extend personal encouragement to his staff. He thought it was fine to communicate only by e-mail," said Heifer's manager of talent development, who gave Birkmans to the team. "He meant well, but his detached impersonal style left his colleagues—with their significantly higher Needs for Esteem scores—feeling frustrated, unappreciated, and generally disconnected from him."

Staff members at headquarters validated from personal knowledge that the Birkman reports were "right on." The Birkman was able to highlight some of the reasons behind the problems within the team.

While ethnic and cultural differences may have complicated things, reported the talent development manager, "the team was also challenged by their communication habits and personal styles." Identifying their needs early on may have helped them understand that their differences aren't obstacles and that these different personal styles can actually be the foundation of a successful and productive team.

The Birkman gives people from different cultures and countries who must work together a good place to start to find common ground and a good way to reject simple labeling. The neutral language allows them to examine themselves and come to terms with behavior and expectations that aren't their own.

9

Are You a Frustrated Maverick in the Workplace?

Freedom and Change

The Freedom Component is different from the typical measures in the Birkman assessment in that it offers a much broader perspective and addresses individuality. Freedom and Challenge are the only two Components that offer such a long view. Where you fall on the Freedom spectrum is a powerful clue to the way you perceive others and yourself, and it is the strongest indicator of your idea of yourself as an independent and individualistic personality.

Those with high Freedom scores revel in marching to the beat of their own drum. They don't know, and don't really care, how most people do things. You often can tell them by the creative way they dress or decorate their offices or homes. High Freedom people can be valuable in workplaces where creative thinking is needed. They can see unique approaches to a sticky problem, and they delight in the unexpected.

Many people are quick to call themselves mavericks. Popular culture, particularly in the United States, often romanticizes and encourages the idea of being a free-thinker and even rebellious. The Birkman helps you discover what level of Freedom truly puts you in your comfort zone.

Those who score lower on the Need for Freedom value traditions in society and understand how most people tend to think. They will be more agreeable and go with the flow. They see importance in fitting in with the majority of good people in society and don't seek ways to be different just for the sake of being different. In the workplace, they will be attuned to policy and procedure, as well as to their colleagues. These folks can readily support team thinking and well-established rules.

Although Freedom has a unique function in the Birkman, it is considered here with the Change Component, which is a measure of restlessness. Are you always on task, or do you prefer plenty of variety in your workday?

High Change people, like high Freedom people, enjoy the unexpected. They prefer shifting and variable schedules. They would probably say they like to multitask, and although this is a topic that has been hotly debated—that is, whether people can ever truly multitask—it is fair to say they are energized by moving rapidly from one focus to another.

Those who report a lower Need for Change accomplish their goals—and even recharge—by being left to stay focused on one endeavor at a time. They prefer fewer distractions and get ruffled and fall into Stress by too many interruptions.

As with each of the other Birkman relational Components, most of us tend toward the average range, meaning that we prefer a balance in our life and work between these two extremes. And as with each Component Need, the Birkman gives a reading on the intensity to which each of us prefers one style or the other for our optimal working conditions.

THE BOSS CLOSES IN

A partner in a large New England accounting firm confessed to his consultant that he had found himself at work becoming "as mad as I've been in several years, and it happened twice in the past few months." The consultant, Richard Rardin, of Connecticut, discovered his client was "off the charts on Freedom." After the two discussed the score, the partner realized that what was upsetting to him was that his manager, who typically had a hands-off, delegative management style, had started to get more involved in all his projects. That insight gave the employee the information he needed to have a healthy discussion with his boss.

"They came to a much better understanding of what was at first a fairly unsettling situation for both of them," says Richard.

THE FREEWHEELING BOSS

The new chief executive at a large Houston hospital was in his post only one month when he realized his direct reports started to become dysfunctional. He asked Birkman consultant Patti Corbett Hansen to help him and his executive team of nine vice presidents and directors get through the leadership transition. "We need to get to know each other better," the new boss told her about his immediate goal.

The CEO knew the staff had to learn how to work effectively with him, but he didn't see any big problems. The staff members, for their part, were feeling unhappy and unproductive, but each was thinking it was his or her own individual dissatisfaction. No one saw a broader issue.

Things had been busy at the hospital when the new chief executive came on board. It was seeing a lot of crisis cases, and that tended to preempt organizational functions, including setting aside time for meetings, allowing staffers to form their own conclusions. "They didn't think their new leader wanted them to be successful, so they started the usual business logic—that he wanted to bring in his own people" and fire the current employees, Patti says.

That defeatist attitude was aggravated by the boss's feeling that a good leader should hit the ground running at a new post. He had decided what his staff needed before he even did any observation or homework on the job.

"The big surprise came as everyone shared their Freedom scores," says the consultant.

The new boss was happy with his score—high Freedom in Usual Behavior and Need scores—and proudly explained that he had a very independent leadership style and wanted a culture where each person who reported to him was trusted to do whatever he or she thought the situation called for to be successful. "After all," Patti recalls him saying, "nobody wants anyone telling them what to do."

In reality, nothing could have been further from the truth. Most of the team members had low Freedom Needs and wanted to have a stable environment with a clear vision, where everyone is kept informed about the rest of the team members' actions and they know where they are headed. They felt the

CEO was sabotaging their success by refusing to tell them what he wanted them to do. In the best of times, things worked collaboratively, but when the staffers felt they didn't have what they needed to succeed individually, it became every man for himself in a quiet and desperate way, Patti says.

The Birkman also showed that the group tended to be low Authority, which signifies low verbal dominance, and so they were silent in their suffering, acting separately outside the workplace. "Several had their résumés in order and had begun a job search," Patti says. "People were worried that the ship was sinking."

The consultant had the group sit around the conference room table and asked each person what he or she needed to be successful. Ninety percent asked that the new CEO give them more clarity, more detail and direction, and more face time.

The CEO's big mistake was one we all often make: assuming that what he needed was what everyone else needed—in his case, a high degree of personal Freedom, Patti says. After that session, she says, the new leader's whole demeanor changed to one in which he wanted to give the team the support they needed, not what he thought they should want. "Hearing the Birkman message helped turn them around," she adds. "I applaud new leaders who take the time to know the individuals. I like the CEO who says, 'And what do you need from me?'"

Afterward, every time a major post was filled, the affected team would be given Birkmans and asked to talk about how the dynamics of the team might change. "It's an organic thing," Patti says about making sure employees' needs are being met, especially during transitions. "The Birkman helps get your attention. It's an early warning system. You have to know what to do to counter blind spots."

AIDING THE RED CROSS

The Freedom Component played an unexpected role in helping the American Red Cross with a herculean hiring problem. The organization was reeling from a series of leadership failures in its operations division for the United States, particularly how to lead its many chapters across the country through needed changes in programs and preparedness. Over a year and a half, the group had hired three vice presidents of operations, who for various reasons didn't work out. The friction was causing huge disruptions at the group's national headquarters in Washington.

"They were developing programs in DC and pushing them out to the different chapters," says consultant Peter Capodice. "They got no chapter buy-in. They just said, 'Here is the new program; implement it.' The relationship was marginal at best."

The organization has a good reputation and an interesting leadership culture, Peter says, in that a lot of its executives are from top private industry positions who have gotten to the point in their careers where they want to give back. Peter saw it as an opportunity to lure talent with broad, high-level experience.

He aligned the Red Cross job requirements for the head of operations position with certain Components, and that led him to zero in on Freedom, which he sees as a key attitudinal Component. His reasoning was that in a highly political and reputable organization, you have to make sure you talk to the right people and go through the right channels, something a low Freedom person might be more likely to do. In contrast, "the high Freedom Usual Behavior scores say, 'I'm just going to go do it and ask forgiveness later.'" That is risky in an organization like the Red Cross, Peter adds.

Peter then gave the Birkman to the hiring team, the executive who would be the new hire's boss, and future team members. In the end, the successful candidate had a rock-bottom low Freedom score for Usual Behavior of 1, and a Need score of 22, "so he had a strong communication style," the consultant says. The candidate, of course, had other good qualities, including good instincts about what the organization needed and how to balance those needs with his strengths in Authority—that is, "when to stand up and when to back down," Peter says.

Scott Conner was that successful leader. He retired in 2010 after a long tenure that included a promotion to senior vice president for preparedness and health and safety services. "The use of the Birkman helped provide a good fit," Scott says. "For me to be at the Red Cross for eleven years at that level was highly unusual. During my time there, I must have had ten bosses and seven presidents."

Before Scott joined the Red Cross, he had spent thirty years in the food industry, working in top-level executive posts in marketing and operations at Campbell Soup, Kentucky Fried Chicken, and Burger King. It was his experience with franchises that caught the attention of the Red Cross leadership.

Once on the job, Scott says he treated the Red Cross chapters as he did his food franchises. He made no executive order until he traveled the country and got to know the chapters and their needs and got local management to buy into headquarters' goals. "Later, I brought in a few people from the chapters for important jobs," he says, "so within a year I had established good relations and credibility. Then we could develop a strategic plan on how to grow the business. It was a terrific experience."

LOOKING FOR CHANGE

People with high Change scores often find office culture stultify-ing and see interruptions and unplanned events as invigorating. They like having plenty of different things to do throughout the day and hope no two days are exactly the same at work.

In Vancouver, Canada, an associate pastor at a Canadian Baptist church had to find a way to meet his strong need for variety and new experiences without disrupting his professional and home lives. He enjoyed teaching—his high Empathy score highlighted his ease with connecting to people—and he was well liked—for the short time people got to know him. But he had a hard time staying in one job.

"He was a teddy bear," consultant Jonathan Michael says, "but he switched churches a lot, mostly out of boredom, and so no one was sure if he'd stick around."

The pastor's constant comings and goings made for a résumé that sent up a red flag despite his successful hires. At home, his wife asked, "What's going on? I'm tired of moving."

What was going on was the church worker had a Change Need score of 90. "He needed people who understood him," Jonathan says. "He needed new challenges and new projects for him to be happy in his job and to stay put." Because the consultant had an established working relationship with the church, he was able to help the pastor negotiate job duties that included a variety of responsibilities and leading the new projects coming up at the church. He took over more counsel-ing tasks from the senior pastor, who, as a strong Yellow, was happy to take on more administrative functions.

"Both are happy doing what they are wired to do better," Jonathan reports. "Rather than focusing on the job description they had to fit, we fit the job description to their Interests and Needs."

KEEP THE CHANGE

Celia Crossley had to coach two low Change executives through some tough restructuring. The leaders of a Midwest manufacturers' group adopted the Birkman after the organization began to feel the strains of the loss of income due to another organization taking away their clients. The membership-driven group was suddenly shrinking in revenue as the economic landscape shifted for small suppliers. The association's office had to trim the pay of the staffers without eliminating any positions.

The chief executive and chief operating officer were beginning to show the signs of stress at work. They were dealing harshly with one another, and that lack of cooperation was making it hard for the staffers to get their work done. The reduced pay added stress and anxiety. Staffers were losing their enthusiasm for work, and overall productively was falling.

Celia gave the executives—and subsequently their entire leadership team—Birkmans. The results showed the CEO and COO were particularly vulnerable to workplace disruptions. The chief executive had an extremely low score for Change, and the operating officer's score was not much higher. That pointed to an extreme desire for predictability—something that was in short supply at the time. The Birkman "differences to watch" segment helped the two executives pinpoint particular problems in their dealings with each other, such as the fact that the CEO appeared to be a flexible planner but in fact needed to have a detailed plan to follow. (His Structure score was Usual Behavior 29 and Needs 66.)

Once the team members began to understand the nature of their emotional strain and were able to identify the behavior that was driving office tension, they could work on an even keel together even without the stable environment they craved. They started to put in place a plan to regain the association's lost income.

"They are in a much better place," says Celia, "not only with a greater understanding of their own behavior, but also of the behavior of their team members. They two led the organization back into stability and it is once again in growth mode."

THE BIRKMAN AT WORK: NONPROFIT ORGANIZATIONS

The Birkman is used by a number of nonprofit organizations. Some 10 percent of the business at Birkman International is in nonprofit activity, including a variety of faith-based groups and large multinationals such as Heifer International. Much of that work is the same being done at any for-profit endeavor: team building, improving work efficiency, and helping bring harmony where conflicts are forming among employees. But clients also have taken remarkable and creative initiative to use the Birkman in ways where finding out a person's true Interests and Needs is of critical importance. These service-oriented organizations use the assessment to get a life back on track, take some of the load off public services, and bring a degree of harmony to a chaotic environment.

Happy Together

Cy Farmer, an international consultant for Cru, has been working for nearly forty years in Africa and Europe for the Christian evangelical group. He uses the Birkman mostly to facilitate training and developing staff, and to help people prepare for jobs in other countries. It also has been invaluable, he says, in helping people "be more effective with the public."

Because one goal of organization members is "to share their faith with others," the Birkman helps individuals understand how they may come across to others and teaches them to be respectful of the other person's needs and perspective. Otherwise, Cy says, "people tend to relate in terms of their own autobiography: 'if it works for me, it should work for others.'"

"The fact that you have five people who love the Lord doesn't mean they work well together," he continues. He can recall one time when two missionaries in Germany were going on a mission trip to an Eastern-European country. One was ready to go in an instant; the other wouldn't leave until all the planning was done. One, in other words, was high in Freedom and low in Structure; the other was low in Freedom and high in Structure. The first person would say, "Let's leave early tomorrow; we'll get there about 11:00 p.m., and we can knock on the pastor's door and he will find a bed for us." The second person would reply, "We aren't leaving this town until we have a written confirmation of a reservation at a local hotel at least three days before we get in the car to go."

Their Stress modes exaggerated how they saw the other person. One saw the other as too anxious and too conforming. The other thought the first person was too unpredictable and individualistic and didn't think things through. Once they saw their Birkman results, they understood what the other person's concerns were and knew they could deal with the differences. "Then they shook hands and walked out of the room with a renewed desire to work and accomplish their mission goals together," Cy says.

The Road Back

Mark Hadley spent most of his adult life in prison on charges including possession of drugs, burglary, and driving while intoxicated. More than a year before his release in 2012 for his fourth sentence, he joined a reentry program at a Texas prison and was given a Birkman by consultant Tommie Dorsett. He was solid Yellow and had high Structure scores, signaling a deep affinity for process and logistics, Tommie says.

It made sense. In prison, Mark was given administrative work, including working for the state highway department as a production clerk, and he always did the work well and happily. He preferred it to any of the construction work he had done on the outside. When he looked at his Birkman results, Tommie recalls, all the prisoner could say was, "Now it makes sense."

"The Birkman showed me way, way more than what I knew about myself," Mark says. "It kept me from thinking I was crazy. All the jobs in my life were blue-collar jobs. I learned that you find yourself a good trade and keep it, and I couldn't get past that. I started drinking to counter the boredom. Then I'd get into trouble, and then I'd have to start all over again. Now I see it."

The consultant works with InnerChange Freedom Initiative, a nondenominational ministry of prison fellowship based in Houston and working mostly in Texas and Minnesota. The organization helps people transition back into society from prison. In Mark's prison, that meant starting with a Birkman. Tommie says he also uses the assessment to help prisoners deal with the stresses of incarceration. "People don't understand their needs and how to communicate that to others," he says, adding that the Birkman helped some prisoners drastically change their behavior.

After Mark was released, at the age of fifty-three, he got help finding a job in charge of operations with a Houston company that does commercial millwork. He is responsible for ensuring that all parts and equipment are ordered properly and arrive on the correct job sites each day at the proper time. "I did procurement for a project for a security desk in an iconic historic building in downtown Houston," he boasts.

He feels the Birkman not only pointed him to the right job, but that it also helped him land it. He says he handed his Birkman results to his prospective boss so he could see his profile, which showed the applicant's preferences as well as suggestions on how to manage him and how he reacted to stress. It showed, for example, that when he began to feel overwhelmed, he would start to do busy work and become unproductive, something Mark says "is so true." More important, he says, it was an independent verification that the type of work he was asking to be hired to do "was my natural ability."

"The Birkman got me to feel that I am capable of doing a job that I have to do," says Mark. His employer agrees, and at his last performance review, Mark got a raise. He has done well enough after eight months on the job that the company is looking to hire another worker from his prison. On a personal level, Mark says he feels relieved. "Since I've been out, I know how to meet my needs," he says.

10

The Wide-Angle View
Challenge

Challenge is the Component that sets the Birkman apart from similar assessments. The Need for Challenge addresses the degree to which we are able to present ourselves to those around us in a positive light. Are you outwardly self-confident, or do you tend to be more outwardly self-critical? Do you exude an easy self-assurance to charm others, or do you charm them by a self-effacing, more self-deprecating style?

It isn't just about the individual, but also about how the individual perceives himself or herself and other people. It shows whether you tend to set yourself up for a series of achievable successes or strive for ever-harder challenges while accepting—even inviting—others' input. Both can be paths to success, but which style works better for you? Of all the characteristics unique to the Birkman, the Challenge score is perhaps the most outstanding in its distinctive ability to measure a fundamental perspective that has an impact on everything we do and say. It is the single important measurement that encompasses all of the relational insights of the Birkman. It is also a self-and-others view that may well be embedded in our core view of ourselves.

Challenge, like Freedom, is also a perspective unlike any of the other Birkman Components. It doesn't follow the three-tiered Usual Behaviors, Needs, and Stress measurements. Challenge is, rather, an overarching perceptual filter and a highly influential one. It provides a valuable piece of information that speaks volumes about a person's outward self-confidence and offers solid clues as to how personally self-critical and demanding a person tends to be.

In the workplace, your approach to Challenge will emerge from your first interview with a company, when you must evaluate yourself. Some of a company's best candidates were not their best interviewees. Birkman has saved more than one job candidate.

Many of us will see a score that lies somewhere in the center, meaning that we find outward self-confidence or self-criticism to be conditional and based on the situation. On the Birkman scale, that means the general population lands between 40 and 60, with an average of a predictable 50. All of us are capable of alternating between the need to project a confident, self-assured demeanor and the temptation to be critical of ourselves.

If you lived alone on an island, how easily you can project self-assurance wouldn't be an issue. But in the real world, Challenge is a useful measure of how you see yourself in the context of society and how you sense others perceive you. You ask yourself, "Do I look successful to other people? Do I feel that I am more than or less than most people?"

Challenge, for example, can point to how your inability to accept praise can be thwarting your image at work. Coaching may be needed to avoid the awkwardness that can follow accolades. When are you being too modest, and when do you need to share more reward and praise with colleagues?

Most successful salespeople and professionals who depend on their talent for communication and persuasion are low Challenge. As an audience, you would want to see the smooth, easy news anchor image of a low Challenge person. They are charming and good at selling themselves. It is important for them to maintain a public image of success, and they are very protective of that image. It can also cause them to publicly deflect blame when things go wrong, even if inwardly they worry the blame might be justified.

Many CEOs score on the lower Challenge side. They project self-confidence and give an air of invincibility, and can easily adapt to socially desirable traits and convey competence. Birkman is seeing more lower Challenge scores in high-performing executives, including at the upper echelons of management. In general, those who fall into the lower end of the continuum tend to set reasonable goals for themselves so there is little to no risk of embarrassing failure.

At the other end of the spectrum, those with a higher Need for Challenge will find it more difficult to sell themselves. They tend to be self-critical and may even blame themselves for things going wrong that they have no control over. They may take on impossible tasks and risk a devastating failure because their drive for accomplishing the difficult (challenging) goals helps them feel better about themselves.

So if you are dealing with others or leading them, how do you help them maintain their desire to be seen in a positive light? How would you coach a very self-assured employee or an overly self-critical one?

LEADERSHIP AND CHALLENGE

Consultant Todd A. Uterstaedt of Cincinnati worked for six months with an executive at a health care organization who was seen as a high-potential manager—a future contender for the company's top post. The organization is a family-owned regional group that caters to senior citizens through a range of services: from in-clinic visits to around-the-clock home care. The group's upper management was beginning to craft a succession plan and was considering Todd's client, a family member in his thirties who was seen as very capable but young for the position—and in need of some coaching.

The Birkman showed that the client had a low Challenge score, which was soon to become central to the preparation training, as well as to the coaching effort itself. Todd had begun by putting together a hefty 360-degree review that included feedback from more than a dozen of the client's colleagues. The consultant was trying to tread lightly on the critiques, knowing that a low Challenge person wants to look good in other people's eyes and tends to dread criticism. "I kept asking him how he was doing as we made it through the report," says Todd, and the client kept telling him to continue.

Later he admitted to Todd that the process was excruciating for him. "It was just too much," he said, joking that he felt like hitting the consultant. But he couldn't tell him to stop because he didn't want him to think less of him.

"Now that gives a true understanding of a low Challenge person!" Todd says.

The two had in-depth discussions about what the low Challenge score represents. Part of that profile is the need to set achievable goals, so the client found a way to absorb constructive criticism from others, "where he wasn't open to that at all before," Todd says.

Today the client has assumed more responsibility, and he gives much credit to the time spent in coaching and, in particular, understanding his low Challenge score.

"Now he thinks about his decisions more deeply and asks whether the decision he has made was done to look good in the eyes of others, or was the best action to take for the sake of the organization," Todd says.

The group is still trying to put a leadership plan in place, and the client is participating in that effort.

NOT YOUR FAULT

Birkman consultant Mary Ruth Burton helped a manager at the other end of the Challenge spectrum. She was coaching an executive in a financial services organization who was getting—unexpectedly—a series of promotions for jobs well done, rising from an individual contributor to a senior director. "She didn't set out to run a good-size area, but they kept adding responsibility to her work," says Mary Ruth. "She developed, almost reluctantly, into a good manager."

The senior director's 98 Challenge score meant a tendency to blame herself for every performance and personality issue in her group. Her understanding demeanor made her popular with her peers, but as she rose to become their boss, she had to learn how to draw boundaries between herself and those she managed. With each individual encounter, she learned and adjusted her perspective. "She became excellent at dealing with her group, helping them understand their strengths and how to leverage them." With coaching, she also learned how to be less hard on herself and came to see that she could make decisions, even difficult ones, about others based on their actions and that those actions had nothing to do with her failures.

LOVING THE CHALLENGE

Atlanta consultant Esther S. Powers decided to use disparate Challenge scores to her advantage when giving a Birkman to a man she had been dating. "I love assessment, so I thought it would be a great way to select who I'd be with" in a relationship, she says.

The man she had been seeing, Tom, took a Birkman, and she saw they looked compatible—except for the Challenge score. "I'm high Challenge; he's low Challenge," she says. "He likes to be appreciated."

"Challenge is often an issue when two people can't get along," she adds. "It's a big deal. Low Challenge people say, 'I want to be seen as successful so I'll do all in my power to make others think that,' to the point of sometimes boasting. A high Challenge person is looking to solve problems: the bigger the better."

The difference became obvious when each was under stress. "I'm a perfectionist and demanding, and I overprepare. I have huge goals for everything, and I want my household run that way too. He's more charming and takes the path of least resistance, and will do things well enough."

She married the man and has adopted his low Challenge way of doing things. Now, she says, she looks at situations and says, "How would Tom do this?"

Pittsburgh consultant Doug Leonard would agree with the power of the Challenge score to solve disputes. He had to help two government engineers end a feud that had become personal, threatening their team's assignment. "Their upstream leader was beyond frustration," says Doug. "Their cooperation was essential to the success of the program." The bad feelings were long-standing and had become institutionalized over time, although they were not based on any professional differences.

The only Birkman scores the consultant introduced into the conversation were for the Challenge Component. One engineer had scored a 6 and the other an 81. "I was able to show them how their misperception of each other grew, particularly under the stress of a high-stakes program," the consultant says. The high Challenge engineer thought the low Challenge engineer was dodging responsibility for problems in the program, and the low-score employee was upset that he was never credited for all of his accomplishments and was tired of attacks on his credibility. "My observation was that they were locked in a fight-to-win cycle, and you could see that in the Birkman: both were high Stress in Authority, Freedom, and Advantage," Doug says. Those scores pointed to their tendencies to escalate a conflict, talk past each other without listening to what the other was saying, and have the last word in an argument.

Doug started a dialogue between the two using the Birkman report. "They were surprised that they had as much in common as they did and how those similarities were highlighted in the report," Doug says. After just one session, he had them agreeing to band together, "albeit toward a common enemy," the consultant adds. "A new alliance was forged." The two had found a way to work together more peacefully.

A LOOK INSIDE

For consultant Patti Corbett Hansen, of Houston, Challenge is the best Component for helping individuals see themselves clearly and goes to the core of how she uses the Birkman.

"I wanted to do something to help people restore faith in themselves," she says. "Instead of looking for someone to ask for help, it answers the question: 'What do you have within you that can help?'" The Birkman, she says, can shine a light on your strengths and help you to see how to become more resilient and trust that you have the resources to solve your own problems.

One of the strengths of the Birkman is that it gives us the ability to see ourselves and our behavioral styles in a social context. In other words, it helps give invaluable answers to a number of questions—such as: How do my day-to-day behaviors or my motivating needs compare with the person I am dealing with at work or outside the office? How am I similar to or different from the others on my team? How do my spouse and I contrast and compare in terms of our interests? How do we differ in terms of what recharges us, or depletes us?

At the end of the day, we want the answers to help understand what we all have within us: a profound human need to be loved and accepted and to find solace and satisfaction by giving love and acceptance to others.

THE BIRKMAN AT WORK: LIFE'S NEXT ACT

Many of us today will live long and healthy lives, we'll have more than one career, and some of us will undertake more than one profession. Sometimes we just need a small departure from our routine as we balance our home and work lives. Those who choose to leave the workplace behind entirely are likely to plan for a life in pursuit of long-held dreams. At all of these junctures, it isn't always clear what the next step looks like. After catering to the demands of others at work and at home for so long, we aren't even sure what we want. The Birkman can reveal to us—or just remind us—of our own motivations and needs so that our next acts can be a better choice for us.

Military, Translated

One of the more difficult and trying transitions into work can be reentry from serving in the military. "A particular type of person is attracted to the military," says Tony Palmer of Atlanta, who specializes in counseling military officers and is a former Navy aviator. In Birkman terms, it often is a person who scores high on a Need for Authority (likes to know who is in charge) with a high Need for Structure (prefers a system and process to be in place) and a lower Need for Freedom (little need to express individuality). Anyone with a nontraditional military profile, he says, would likely become a pilot or a member of Special Forces—the kinds of occupations that allow less Structure and more Freedom.

No matter how they serve, however, military personnel tend to share the same transition issue when they leave to enter the mainstream workplace. "They are suddenly faced with an extraordinary amount of freedom where they had no freedom in the past," says Tony.

All else being equal, one of the biggest hurdles the return-ing veteran faces is that it isn't always easy to match a civilian position with prior military responsibilities. That disconnect can hinder the résumé-writing and job-search process. "The prob-lem is translation—their experience is in language and responsi-bilities that civilians don't readily understand," Tony says.

To address that issue, Birkman International, in addition to the usual assessment report, provides a "crosswalk," a listing of correlations between military and civilian jobs to guide mili-tary job seekers and the companies who are hiring them. "The value of the Birkman is to help military people understand where their natural gifts and strengths are, which is critical to identifying and securing their best options," he says.

Tony coached one army officer who had served for eight years in his post, earning a record of strong accomplishment in data and records management. An initial challenge for him when he was first looking for civilian employment was to translate his extensive experience into meaningful civilian language. He managed to do that by matching his experience with the job descriptions in the Birkman Job Families Report, Tony says. He also used his Birkman Usual Behavior scores to highlight his strengths in eleven themes of work during interviews with recruiters and hiring managers. He was able to land a job within several months as a senior manager of record services for a major municipality at a six-figure salary, Tony says. Dennis M. Orr of Golden, Colorado, a former Air Force captain, says many veterans are reluctant even to speak about what they were doing in the services, let alone to discuss equivalent civilian jobs. "You don't necessarily want to keep doing what you had to do in the military," he says, "you want to move into what you want to do."

Many of the people he coaches have suffered physical and mental traumas during their wartime tours of duty, he says. In those cases, the Birkman has helped him teach about potential Stress triggers. But veterans, in general, can feel thrown by the loss not only of the structure they crave, but also of the camaraderie and high level of accountability that come with military work, the consultant adds. He led a group of unemployed members of the Colorado National Guard, and spouses, through a pilot employment project in October 2012. Two months after the first twelve participants completed the four-week course, two already had found new jobs. Dennis credits the Birkman with contributing to the success of the course: a forty-hour workshop that began with the assessment and went on to teach resume-writing and interviewing techniques, among other things.

One participant, a veteran in his forties, had retired from the military after more than twenty years, and had an expertise in languages and in intelligence. It was no surprise when the Birkman showed he had a high Interest in Literary, as well as strengths in Persuasion and Mechanical. As is typical with military personnel, he had a high Usual Behavior score for Structure and he was deeply Red. He landed a federal government job in Colorado with the Air Force. He told Dennis that the Birkman gave him "great insights" during the job search, and that he expected to continue to refer to his report throughout his new career.

The Enjoyment/Employment Pattern

Betsy Cole, PhD, of Waltham, Massachusetts, knows how hard it can be to get to a second act in a career. She helps women, in particular, figure out what the next phase of their professional life might be and how to make it more rewarding than previous work. She combines the Birkman with other exercises to get people to see their unique gifts "and the work they were born to do."

She likes to talk to them about their success stories over their lifetimes to uncover themes and patterns that might lead to their fulfillment and success. "A job is an expression of a pattern," she says, "especially in the second half of life. They may not even have a job, but they do things for fun. It's an expression of who they are."

One woman in her mid-fifties with three grown children was in a corporate job in a pharmaceutical company but was starting to feel stuck. She described her role as being a "helpmate" to her boss. She worked behind the scenes to aid his success, but the question dogged her: "What is *my* life purpose?"

Her Birkman showed her to be a strong Blue, someone who wanted to delve into long-term strategies and planning, not taking on a management role. She also was profiled as a knowledge specialist or a consultant. She discovered using the Birkman and other tools that she wanted to leave her operations position and move into one that drew on her scientific experience of helping to bring new drugs to market. She had never been good at going after what she wanted, partly because that was never clear to her. With coaching, she began to have more conversations at the company about her needs and what opportunities were available to her. She made specific requests, told her superiors what she was looking for, and engaged her mentors in discussion. Over time, she was offered a job that required her to step up and be a leader in her own right. She is continuing to look to even better opportunities and is getting closer to her dream job as a strategic leader in helping to identify promising scientific research that can spur the development of crucial new drugs.

Retire or Rewire?

Bob Brewer coached one woman as she looked to leave behind a career as a senior tax accountant. "She said, 'I'm fifty, and I don't know if I should stay in accounting.' She was in a midlife crisis, fighting boredom," says Bob.

She told him she had always wanted to be a librarian, but her father told her when she was young that the best way for girls to make money was in accounting. When Bob and his client looked at her Birkman together, it was not a surprise that she had a literary Interest score in the 90s. "If you get above 90, it's a passion, and you better be involved in that in some way," he told her.

The woman decided after much thought and counseling that she was "too deep in her career" to make a job change or retire early. In that case, the consultant advised her to make a smaller but no less important change: volunteer at a library. She did, and tending to her real needs made her feel content enough that she was able to continue in her career.

An American theologian working overseas for thirty-nine years wasn't ready to retire either, but in 2012 he started planning his reentry into the United States. At age sixty-eight, Trent Hyatt and his wife, Vivian, were preparing to begin a new phase in life and wondered about the best way to approach the lifestyle choices they faced. The missionary was teaching church history, theology, and the Bible in Eastern Europe and Russia. When he was working in Budapest, he and his team were given Birkmans by consultant Cy Farmer in Germany. Trent had an unexpectedly high score in music. He said he always had music playing in his office but had never focused on it. Now he was excited to explore what this discovery might mean in the context of his future plans.

"I do have a passionate love for classical music," says Trent. "But that is a hobby or just one of my loves. I also love nature, mountains, the ocean, and so on. I have a PhD in systematic theology, and I am a teacher. I love to teach. So it never even occurred to me that music would show up as my highest value. What was funny to me was the way everyone, *everyone* else on the team, said, 'Of course! We knew that.'"

He said the assessment helped him realize "and accept" that "to experience life with a satisfying balance and pleasure, I need music—lots of it. Knowing this has, in a way, released me to indulge this beautiful passion without feeling somehow guilty about it. It is part of me, part of what makes me, me."

The Birkman helped lead him to the idea that the next home he and his wife would share would be in an area where music, concerts, and musical education could be a substantial part of their everyday lives.

Epilogue

Do People Change?

Do people change? This is a good question and one frequently asked of Birkman consultants. People often want to take the Birkman more than once because they feel certain that their scores will have changed over the years. We usually tell them that it isn't really necessary. The Birkman is a robust assessment and tends to remain statistically reliable although we continue to monitor such results.

Our Interests are apparent from an early age and generally remain consistent over a lifetime. Needs are part of our core personality and also tend to be steady over time, even if we appear to have changed over the years. What matters is that we change what we *can* change, and what we can change is our awareness. Where socialized behaviors are concerned, we have amazing abilities to determine, decide, adapt, develop, and, to a great extent, choose our behaviors. With heightened awareness, we can exercise significant control over our personalities in social interactions. This is one reason we may see a person we know to be quiet and reserved come across in certain situations as surprisingly outgoing; or a person who has been overbearing learn to listen.

In Birkman terms, we can *consciously modify how we choose* to "show up" when we relate to others. We can shift and adapt our outward daily (Usual) behaviors, even though the essential, innermost part of us (our Needs and Interests) will not change much over time. With understanding, we can adopt behaviors that are more effective in our personal or working environments. The Birkman assessment's revelations about your Interests, Needs, and Usual Behaviors can be vital to helping you achieve fulfillment while showing you how to minimize your negative Stress behaviors. This is why Birkman International loves what it does. As you've seen in the examples throughout this book, when we gain understanding of ourselves and others, we can make positive changes. From this perspective of greater compassion and understanding, we believe people do change, and for the better.

What we cannot change—and should never want to change—is the essence of who we are. It's easy to see in nature when we consider the example of a tree. An oak will always be an oak. No amount of coaching or assessing will ever morph the oak into a pine tree, and no matter how much its appearance changes, its basic "oakness" remains. From acorn to mature tree, it forever bears the DNA of an oak because that's what it was meant to be.

A central message from the Birkman is that all of us have personality traits and interests that offer value to our family, team, organization, and society as a whole. We encourage everyone to embrace their combination of traits and take care to get their own Interests and interpersonal Needs met. What Birkman uniquely measures are those powerful internal core Needs—the part of us that others do not easily see yet are an essential part of who we are. These Needs that we call

Components function for us like the complex underground root system of the oak tree, and like the roots of the oak, they anchor, nourish, and recharge us. Getting our interpersonal Needs met may seem easier. We know it's easy to fall into the Stress behaviors that are the inevitable flip side of our strengths. When it comes to seeing our own personality, the Birkman can serve as our mirror, enabling us to see those parts of ourselves that are not easy for us to see on our own.

So we go back to the question about whether people change. Well, yes, they do. Even if our core doesn't change, we see important behavioral changes happen when people make better choices because they view themselves and others in a new way. With better choices, we become more emotionally intelligent with the kind of self-awareness that enables better self-management. When we know ourselves and understand and appreciate others, we flourish. Will it look as if we've changed? Absolutely!

Relationships make and break companies, and not one of us succeeds alone or thrives in isolation. Leadership also is important because the reality is that each of us is a leader, whether it is a large organization, a small team, a family, or, most important, ourselves, that we lead. We seek a way to relate every day to everyone who comes in contact with us.

Birkman is grateful to have studied and worked with so many people over six decades and will continue to do so because we see people change and grow when they see themselves and others in a nonjudgmental light that is kind, bright, and objective. With self-awareness, you can know your strengths, see your value, and learn how to reach comfort and fulfillment in being exactly who you truly are!

Interviewees

Stephanie Capparell interviewed the following people in a series of conversations and e-mails from October 2010 to January 2013:

Dave Agena, founder/chairman, P.A.S.S. Coaching, Laguna Niguel, California

Stephan Altena, PhD, ISHR Group, Munich, Germany

Wendy Andreen, PhD, senior certified Birkman consultant, Houston, Texas

Karen Armstrong, vice president, Diversity and Leadership Development, Tyson Foods Inc., Springdale, Arkansas

Ron Baker, senior Birkman consultant, Pentecostal Assemblies of Canada, Western Ontario District, Burlington, Ontario, Canada

Janice Bergstresser, executive consultant and coach, Take Charge, Coatesville, Pennsylvania

Roger Birkman, PhD, designer of Birkman assessment tool and founder of Birkman International Inc., first interviewed at headquarters, Houston, Texas, October 8, 2010

Bob Bolling, senior Birkman consultant, The Personality Coach, Houston, Texas

Jan Brandenbarg, Birkman consultant, Ambt Delden, the Netherlands

Bob Brewer, PhD, senior certified Birkman consultant, Leadership and Teamwork Institute, Oxford, Mississippi

Mary Ruth Burton, president, Burton-Fuller Management, Richmond, Virginia

Jenny Capella, Birkman consultant and owner, Capella Group, Seattle, Washington

Peter Capodice, senior certified Birkman consultant and president, Capodice & Associates Predictive Performance Executive Search, Sarasota, Florida

Claire Carrison, president, Millvale, Camden, South Carolina, and Cuernavaca, Mexico

Connie Charles, chief executive officer, Strategic Solutions International, Newark, Delaware

Betsy Cole, PhD, principal, Cole Coaching and Consulting, Waltham, Massachusetts

Scott Conner, senior vice president, preparedness, American Red Cross, retired, Naples, Florida

Steve Cornwell, president, Responsibility Centered Leadership, Atlanta, Georgia

Michael Corrao, chief operating officer, CD One Price Cleaners, Westchester, Illinois

Celia Crossley, managing partner, Crosworks/Celia D. Crossley & Assoc., Columbus, Ohio

Suzanne A. Davis, participant in a marriage group at St. Luke's Methodist Church, Houston, Texas

Tommie Dorsett, executive director, Innerchange Freedom Initiative, Richmond, Texas

Holly Dunning, interim manager of talent development, Heifer International, Little Rock, Arkansas

Cy Farmer, international representative, Cru, Kandern, Germany

Beroz Ferrell, partner, The Point, Kent, Washington

Steven Foster, area manager, Redefine Hotel Management, London, UK

Randi Gregoire, Birkman consultant, Orlando, Florida

Mark Hadley, manager, Soli Deo Gloria House, Houston, Texas

Jeffrey P. Haggquist, DO, QuistMD, Washington, DC

Shelley Hammell, president, Sage Alliance, Atlanta, Georgia

Patti Corbett Hansen, Birkman consultant, Houston, Texas

Lisa Hart, human resources consultant, ISHR Group, Boston, Massachusetts

Robert Hudson, president, M&H Marketing, Louisville, Kentucky

D. Trent Hyatt, PhD, director, Institute for Biblical and Theological Studies, Budaörs, Hungary

Philippe Jeanjean, director, development and technology, Boston Global, Boston, Massachusetts

Amelia Jeffers, president and co-owner, Garth Auctions, Delaware, Ohio

Bayley Kessler, chief executive officer, Joailliere Designs, Lacey, Washington

John B. Lazar, president, John B. Lazar & Associates, Forest Park, Illinois

Doug Leonard, director of consulting services, Strategic Solutions International, Pittsburgh, Pennsylvania

Stacey Mason, owner, Mason On Leadership, Bentonville, Arkansas

Jonathan Michael, principal, Foresight Leadership Solutions, Vancouver, Canada

Anne Morriss, founder and chief knowledge officer, Concire Leadership Institute, Cambridge, Massachusetts

Al-karim Nathoo, associate director, 4C Hotel Group, London, England

Dennis M. Orr, president and chief executive officer, Colorow Consulting, Golden, Colorado

Tony Palmer, director, Stanton Chase International, Atlanta, Georgia

Ervis Duardo Perez, MD, participant in Birkman Discovery Workshop for Couples, Milton, Ontario, Canada

Esther S. Powers, PhD, chief executive officer, E. Powers & Associates, Atlanta, Georgia

Richard Rardin, president, BenchStrength Development LLC, Sandy Hook, Connecticut

Joanne Rivard, vice president for human resources, IPEX Management, Mississauga, Ontario

Tamara Pina Riverón, participant in Birkman Discovery Workshop for Couples, Milton, Ontario, Canada

Barbara Robinson, principal, Robinson & Associates, Washington, DC

Patricia A. Russell, president, Russell Consulting Group, Park City, Utah

Dana Scannell, PhD, president, Scannell & Wight, Newport Beach, California

Sonya Shields, executive national vice president and independent consultant, Arbonne, DeWinton, Canada

Stacy L. Sollenberger, partner and executive coach, ISHR Group, Atlanta, Georgia

Tony Swift, general manager, human resources, Hyundai Motor Company, Sydney, Australia

Ulanda Terry, director, Diversity and Leadership Development, Tyson Foods, Springdale, Arkansas

Nancy Thompson, organizational effectiveness and human resource manager, Procter & Gamble, Cincinnati, Ohio

Todd A. Uterstaedt, president and chief operating officer, Baker & Daboll, Cincinnati, Ohio

Tasneem Virani, director, Claris Coaching, London, England

Phillip Weiss, principal, P.A. Weiss, Houston, Texas

Karyl White, energy attorney and participant in Birkman Discovery Workshop for Couples, Houston, Texas

Ian Whitfield, cofounder, Right Foot Green, Calgary, Alberta, Canada

Wilson Wong, president and chief executive officer, Wilson Wong & Associates, Alpharetta, Georgia

Carleen and Bob Woods, participants in Birkman Discovery Workshop for Couples, Houston, Texas

Notes

Introduction

1. Roger Birkman, *True Colors* (Houston: Birkman International, 1995), xix.
2. Warren Bennis, *Still Surprised: A Memoir of a Life in Leadership* (San Francisco: Jossey-Bass, 2010), 55.

Chapter 1

1. Michael J. Leonard, "Major Decisions," March 12, 2010, http://dus.psu.edu/md/mdintro.htm.

Chapter 2

1. Norwood Teague, e-mail to Mary Ruth Burton, October 29, 2012.

Chapter 5

1. Shannon Woolard, e-mail to Steve Cornwell, March 2011.

Acknowledgments

We offer our genuine thanks to our agent, Giles Anderson, who started this book when he reached out to us with an idea, and to Karen Murphy, our editor at Jossey-Bass, who offered expert guidance and the ideal home for a Birkman book.

Our deep gratitude to the Birkman consultants who provided their stories for this book, and to all the Birkman colleagues whose work has improved the lives and workplaces of so many people over the years and across the world.

About the Authors

SHARON BIRKMAN FINK is president and CEO of Birkman International, developer of the Birkman Method. She took over as head of the company in 2002 in a planned management transition for the company, which was founded in 1951 by her father, Dr. Roger Birkman. For more information, please visit www.birkman.com.

STEPHANIE CAPPARELL is a New York–based journalist, author, and filmmaker. She has worked for more than twenty years at the *Wall Street Journal*, where she is an editor and writer. She is the author of the international bestseller *Shackleton's Way* and *The Real Pepsi Challenge*.

Index

Page numbers in italics refer to figures.

About Birkman International, Inc.

BIRKMAN INTERNATIONAL, INC., is a publisher of online assessment services. Birkman's focus is on the development and distribution of scientifically developed tests and assessments with strong integrity, reliability, and validity. Since 1951, Birkman's services have been used by thousands of organizations, thousands of professional consultants, and millions of people worldwide. This global community uses Birkman to develop better leadership, promote more effective teamwork, find meaningful careers, improve hiring, and generate increased levels of performance and well-being for individuals, teams, and organizations.

The Birkman Method®
An assessment of behavior, motivation, and occupational preference with over thirty reports that can be produced to facilitate coaching, leadership development, team building, career counseling, career outplacement, hiring, and conflict management.

The Birkman 360° survey

A multi-rater survey of nine leadership behaviors that can be used alone or combined with The Birkman Method. The results provide a foundation for individual coaching by identifying opportunities for development.

The Birkman Abilities Inventory

A general reasoning assessment measuring problem identification and problem solving. The results are used principally within hiring and selection activities.

Consulting Services

A global network of independent Birkman consultants is available to provide you with Birkman-based services. Contact Birkman (info@birkman.com) to find a qualified consultant near you.

Birkman's goal is to develop valid, reliable assessments that can be used to make better hires, develop more effective leaders, improve teamwork, achieve more meaningful careers, and generate higher levels of individual and team performance and well-being. For more information, please contact sales@birkman.com or call 1-800-215-2760.